D0805560

this book belongs to

Meredith Fowler

Frontispiece:
TEMPLE OF KALABSHA
Detail of facade.
Reign of Ptolemy IX Soter II, 88-81 B.C.
Originally situated about 25 miles
south of Assuan Dam, the temple has
been moved to a location near the dam.

TREASURES
OF THE NILE

TREASURES OF THE NILE

Art of the Temples and Tombs of Egypt

by Kamal El Mallakh
with Robert Bianchi

Newsweek /NEW YORK

Editorial Director:
Henry A. La Farge

Organizational plan:
Kamal El Mallakh

Introduction by:
Robert S. Bianchi

Commentary texts by:
Robert S. Bianchi

Published by
NEWSWEEK, INC.
& KODANSHA LTD. TOKYO

This volume is being published simultaneously under
the title *Museums of Egypt*

Library of Congress Cataloging in Publication Data

Mallākh, Kamāl El.
    Treasures of the Nile.

    Bibliography: p. 169
    Includes index.
    1. Egypt — Antiquities. 2. Egypt — Civilization —
To 332 B.C. 3. Art, Egyptian. I. Bianchi, Robert Steven,
1943-   joint author. II. La Farge, Henry Adams,
1902-   III. Title.
DT56.9.M34   709'.32   80-80044
ISBN 0-88225-293-3

Printed and bound in Japan by
Dai Nippon Printing Company, Tokyo

PREFACE

It was for a long time the dream of Kamal El Mallakh to do a book on the extraordinary wealth of art surviving from Ancient Egypt. With the idea that the famous sites of the Nile Valley today collectively constitute one great museum, it was Mallakh who conceived and realized this project. By organizing a team of photographers to visit the famous temples and tombs and directing them in the selection of the subjects to be reproduced in this volume, Mallakh provided the basis for this important survey and the exquisite color-plates which accompany the commentary texts.

A well-known name in Egypt, Kamal El Mallakh has long been actively engaged in Egyptology. Trained both in archaeological research and as an architect, he was instrumental in 1954 in discovering the *Solar Boat* at Giza illustrated and discussed in these pages. In the 1960's he served on the UNESCO Committee to salvage the Nubian monuments threatened by the rising waters from the Assuan Dam. At the present time, as Deputy Editor-in-Chief and Member of the Board of Editors of *Al-Ahram*, the oldest and most widely circulated newspaper in the Middle East, he is a regular contributor to *Al-Ahram*, with a column reporting on every aspect of Egypt's archaeological riches.

More than simply making a record of his country's monuments, sculptures, and paintings, it was Mr. Mallakh's desire to document the pervasive influence of Ancient Egypt on the West. It is sincerely hoped that this wish has been fulfilled and that Western Man's outstanding debt to that great civilization of Antiquity is acknowledged in these pages.

Editor

INTRODUCTION

ROBERT S. BIANCHI

Associate Curator of Egyptian and Classical Art
The Brooklyn Museum

The wonders of ancient Egypt simultaneously fascinated and confounded the ancient Greeks, who considered themselves the sole bearers of culture; they went to great lengths to disassociate themselves from the remaining peoples of the ancient world. The Greeks, however, could not reconcile their own self-importance with their observation that Egypt, admittedly of greater antiquity than any Greek city-state, was, in her own way, a highly developed civilization which exerted a profound influence on some of the most important figures in Greek history. In the arts, sciences, and philosophy, the Greeks openly admitted their indebtedness to the ancient Egyptians. There is little doubt that the earliest monumental sculpture in Greece, representing the *kouros*, a nude youth, with arms held at his sides and left foot advanced, is a Hellenic adaptation of the canonical Egyptian statuary type of the striding male figure. Rhoecus and Theodorus, architects of the earliest sanctuary of Hera on the Greek island of Samos, based their designs on the multicolumned temples they encountered in Egypt. Although little remains of that temple today, Theodorus wrote a book in the early sixth century B.C. in which that temple is discussed. The book, now lost, is known from citations preserved in the writings of the Romans Vitruvius and Pliny.

The fame of the Egyptians as physicians was well-known in antiquity. Darius the Great (521–486 B.C.) the mightiest king of the Persian Empire, enlisted an Egyptian as his personal physician and is reported to have founded a school of medicine at the Egyptian city of Saïs in the Delta. The Greeks themselves acknowledged the superiority of the Egyptians in medicine. Hippocrates, the so-called father of medicine, although a Greek, is believed to have served an internship in Egypt where he gained exposure to the millennia-old practices of the ancient Egyptians. The famous medical school on the Greek island of Cos and its cult of the Greek healing god Aesculapius were indebted to the philanthropic interests of the Ptolemies who acted as pharaohs of Egypt.

In the field of philosophy, in which the ancient Greeks are universally acclaimed as the masters, Egyptian influence is noticeably detectable. Solon, perhaps the wisest of the Athenians, visited Egypt in the sixth century B.C. and was much impressed by what he saw there. Pythagoras of Samos, who eventually emigrated to Croton, Italy, visited Egypt in the sixth century B.C. as well. Initiated into the mysteries of the Egyptian religion, he is reputed to have evolved his theories about the transmigration of souls from the Egyptian concepts of the travels of the deceased through the Underworld. Plato himself did visit Egypt in the fourth century B.C. Strabo, writing about the turn of the millennium, was shown the buildings at Heliopolis in which Plato was reported to have lived and worked. Plato's concept of the imperishability of the being was, in part, formulated with the help of the mythical gestures of eternity revealed to him by the priests of Egypt's sanctuaries. A group of still unpublished mythical papyri in our collections at The Brooklyn Museum are conjectured to have been written at the time of Plato's visit to Egypt.

When Ptolemy, the son of Lagus, a trusted general of Alexander the Great, seized Egypt as his share of the empire and founded in 305 B.C. the dynasty which bears his name, Alexandria became a center for learning and for theology. Her library was world-famous and the scholars appointed to its staff attempted to collect a copy of every known written work. Many texts in foreign languages were translated into Greek. The historian Manetho, who worked for Ptolemy II, composed a history in Greek of the pharaohs of ancient Egypt relying heavily on Egyptian temple records. Under the reign of that king, the Hebrew scriptures, which were later to be called *The Old Testament*, were translated into Greek for the first time. The Greek world now became exposed to the Judaic traditions. As time passed, Egypt played a significant role in the history of the early Church. The pharaonic image of Isis nursing the child Horus was translated into Christian iconography as the Virgin and Christ Child.

The attraction which Egypt had for the ancient Greeks went beyond a superficial admiration for her monuments. Nonetheless, her monuments, as presented in this volume, can be used as a bridge between our generation and those of the ancient Egyptians, since our world is also indebted to that of the ancient Egyptians. Today, our cities and capitals are endowed with buildings based on classical motifs. Yet, as we will see in this volume, the use of fluted columns and of a precursor of the Greek Doric order are already well established in the architectural idiom of the ancient Egyptians at Saqqara and at Beni Hasan. Our municipal buildings are often provided with water spouts in the form of heads of lions. These gargoyles were invented by the ancient Egyptians who considered rain the results of typhonic powers. An elaborate mythology was evolved—as recorded on the walls of the Temple of Edfu—by which these guardian lions ingested the rain which, thus rendered impotent, was regurgitated beyond the walls of the sanctuary. The Greeks borrowed the form, abandoned its associations, and bequeathed the lion-headed water spout to the West. Architects of the West's Industrial Revolution sought a visual vocabulary which would make new-fangled engineering projects palatable to a skeptical public. Suspension bridges were a novelty in the 1830s; few would dare cross any chasm on gossamer ribbons of metal. To dispel such fears, Brunel masked his suspension bridge at Bristol, England, in 1831 with motifs adopted from Egyptian pylons and temples. Egypt's architectural idiom connoted stability and permanence and, by transferring selected motifs to his own architectural scheme, Brunel played upon the public's conditioned response to Egyptian architecture and thereby achieved his goal.

The connotations of stability and permanence were not limited to such structures. As social systems developed, the need to incarcerate those individuals who acted in socially unacceptable ways required an architectural idiom compatible with that function. During the 1800s, numerous prisons were designed which relied heavily upon Egyptian motifs. Walter's design for the Moyamensing Debtor's Prison in Philadelphia (1832–35) incorporates disparate elements into an imposing facade. Haviland's design of the New Jersey State Penitentiary in Trenton (1832–36) is a remarkable synthesis of elements drawn from Egyptian temples and pylons. The most remarkable of these prisons, however, is that of the "Tombs," designed by Haviland for New York City (1835–1838). It is undoubtedly the most ambitious and most important example of the Egyptian revival in the United States. It incorporates many elements from Egyptian temples presented in this volume and known to Haviland from publications of these monuments which he owned. The Temple of Medinet Habu (p. 99) and that on Elephantine provided him with certain concepts which he incorporated into his plan.

During the 1800s, the United States experienced a spectacular growth in cemeteries. Architects and city planners seized upon Egyptian motifs as the ideal idiom for these eternal resting places. Entrances to Westminster Cemetery in Baltimore (1813–1815), Mount Auburn Cemetery, in Cambridge, Massachusetts (1831), and Grove Street Cemetery in New Haven (1844–1849) employ an Egyptian architectural idiom entirely compatible with the function of the fields onto which they open.

The uniquely Egyptian schema for depicting their own world in two dimensions was repudiated by the Greeks who are responsible for introducing to the West their own visual vocabulary. Despite the hold that idiom has had on the West, many artists of the nineteenth century, searching to break free from traditional concepts, turned to ancient Egypt for inspiration. The predilection of the Post-Impressionists for flattening the picture plane and negating the illusion of depth led to a renewed interest in Egyptian pictorial representations. Gauguin himself based the compositional concerns of *Ta Matete*, painted in 1892, on those found in the tomb of Nakht (p. 127), photographs of which he owned. In addition to flattening out the space, he here experimented with the repeated gestures of the hands, used to unify the surface of the work.

These examples of Egypt's influence on the nineteenth century are limited to the visual arts and serve merely to illustrate the pervasive but often completely ignored influence of Egypt on the beginning of the modern era. We would be remiss, however, if we did not indicate that the ancient Egyptians were, in some respects, similar to us. The significance of their cultural heritage for our own generation is not to be limited to these external borrowings. It is to be hoped that these ever-present visual reminders will motivate some to probe under the surface and begin to understand and appreciate the psyche of the Egyptians themselves. Their literature is extensive and only now is it becoming more readily available in exacting English translations. These compositions, when viewed in conjunction with Egypt's visual legacy, help to provide a more complete picture of the ancient Egyptians as people.

The lure of adventure and the encounters of a hero with the unknown in far-off lands has been a staple of Western literature since Homer's *Odyssey*. This lure was shared by the Egyptians as well. Their *Shipwrecked Sailor* has often been described as a precursor of both Odysseus and Sinbad the Sailor. Casting off from Egypt with a crew of the best sailors in the land, our anonymous hero encounters a storm of a typhoon's proportions, which sinks his craft, drowns his crew, and casts him upon the shores of a fantastic island, provided, like Eden, with all the fruits of the earth necessary for his sustenance. In a few days' time, terror grips our hero as he comes face to face with the island's master, a bearded serpent of behemothic size who speaks Egyptian. Benign by nature and sympathetic to the sailor's plight, the serpent, after cataloguing his own genealogy, predicts the safe return of the sailor, on whom he bestows all the gifts of the island. On the appointed day, a ship from Egypt finds its way to the island, and picks up the sailor and his gifts. Within the best traditions of most of our own 'grade B' science fiction movies, the sailor and his ship sail away from the island just before it sinks beneath the waves of the sea forever!

Sinuhe, the hero of a tale with the same name, leaves Egypt for a voluntary exile, upon over-hearing a secret dispatch about the assassination of his sovereign. His peregrinations in what must certainly be the Syria-Palestine region bring him into contact with the indigenous population, who appear to observe dietary laws similar to those practiced by the Hebrews. The Hebraic element is again observable when Sinuhe, after marrying a local sheikh's daughter, defends his new tribe against a rival by engaging in hand-to-hand combat against a giant, in the tradition of David and Goliath. This Hebraic connection is again found in *The Tale of Two Brothers*, written during the New Kingdom. The basic plot and characters are essentially those found in the *Old Testament*'s story of Joseph and Potiphar's wife.

The love songs of the Egyptians (written during the New Kingdom when Egypt was at her height) reveal the universal affections shared by men for women. The anxiety of the lover walking down the street where his mistress lives, the daydreams and reveries of times past spent together, the asseverations that no woman can compare to his own, the despair of separation, are all expressed in human terms which evoke the empathy of a modern reader.

Despite the apparent absence of law codes, such as known from Mesopotamia during Hammurabi's reign, the Egyptians seem to have established and subscribed to a very strict ethical standard which is revealed to us by the corpus generally known as Wisdom Literature. Socially acceptable behavior, the accepted norms governing man's interaction with man, and caveats about excesses, appear time and again in these treatises. *The Wisdom of Ptah-hotep* and *The Instructions of Kageminy* offer a series of such maxims or precepts covering a broad spectrum of subjects. The excerpts* which follow serve to illustrate the relevance of that advice today:

> Hold thyself in esteem and do not slander anyone. Rely only upon the truth and do not exaggerate. Never repeat words spoken in anger and refrain from maligning any person, regardless of his station in life.
>
> He who is a glutton is a feeble man; if you are invited to dine with a glutton, eat only after his appetite is sated. If you drink with a drunkard, likewise drink only after his thirst is slaked.
>
> Strive to be laconic. It is more beneficial than any other trait. Speak only when you know and fully understand the discussion. Babbling is more irksome than performing the most menial of tasks.
>
> If you are a leader, learn to listen. Do not interrupt a victim of injustice until he has completed what he has to say.

Some indications of accepted modes of behavior are also preserved in the "Chapter of Negative Confessions" from the *Book of the Dead*. The deceased is asked a series of questions about activities in which he is not supposed to have engaged. He asserts:

> I have not harmed animals; I have not known evil; I have not acted wickedly; I have not despised God; I have not caused misery. I have not caused pain. I have not killed. I have not stolen. I have not poached. I have not carried off milk from the mouths of infants.

In many respects, these sentiments echo the *Ten Commandments* and place the ancient Egyptians much closer to the Judeo-Christian ethos than is generally admitted.

With the emergence of Egypt as a Republic in 1953 and the events of recent years in the Middle East, interest in Egypt and in her past are at an all-time high. Special exhibitions of her treasures at museums throughout America have played to record-breaking audiences; new exhibitions are, even at this writing, being planned. New York City has established itself as the center for the purchase of Egyptian works of art as established dealers and auction houses alike experience an ever-increasing volume of sales. The combined collections of The Metropolitan Museum of Art's Egyptian Department and those of our own Department at The Brooklyn Museum offer an unparalleled opportunity for the enjoyment and appreciation of the artistic legacy of Egypt's glorious past.

It is my sincere wish that this volume will acquaint its reader with some of the wonders ancient Egypt has to offer, will impart some aesthetic appreciation of those monuments, and will make the Egyptians appear less distant, less mysterious, and less elusive than they might ordinarily appear to be.

Robert S. Bianchi

*Translated from original texts by the author.

I CAIRO, GIZA, SAQQARA

ISLAMIC CAIRO

Egyptian legend records that the God Horus, attempting to avenge the murder of his father Osiris, fought one of his battles against his archrival Seth in the vicinity of Heliopolis, today a suburb of Cairo. The area was settled by Greek colonists, who called their foundation Babylon. The strategic location of that colony was realized by the Romans, who fortified its citadel with one of the three principal garrisons stationed in Egypt. The fortress prospered until A.D. 639 when Amr ibn es-As, commanding the troops of the Caliph Omar, took Babylon. He transferred the fortress to nearby Fostat, whose ruins can still be visited in Old Cairo. The founding of modern Cairo in A.D. 969 is attributable to a general and to the planet Mars. The Fatimid General Gohar, whose forces wrested Egypt from the Abbasids, decided to build a city to rival Baghdad, capital of the defeated Abbasids. He named it El Qahireh, Arabic for "The Victorious," since the start of its construction coincided with the ascent of Mars, El Qaher in

Below right
EL-AZHAR MOSQUE
970–972 A. D.
Cairo.
Shi'ite Fatimid Caliphate.

Below
AHMED IBN TULUN MOSQUE
876–879 A. D.
Cairo.
Abbasid Caliphate.

Arabic. Since that time Egypt has developed a dialect of Arabic which, while having much in common with the language of the Moslem world, remains distinctly Egyptian. Likewise her architecture, while typically Islamic, remains decidedly Egyptian in character. Unlike Baghdad, and later Damascus and Cordova, Cairo was a center of the Shi'ite sect of Islam. This isolated her in certain respects from the rest of the Islamic world, and fostered the creation of her particular architectural idiom.

AHMED IBN TULUN MOSQUE. *Abbasid Caliphate.* *p. 17*

According to legend, the Mosque of Ibn Tulun was built on a plan drafted by a manumitted Christian captive. He based his design on that of the Kaaba in Mecca. This is virtually the only mosque in Cairo which appears as it did when it was erected in A.D. 876–879. The date of its foundation is preserved in a marble inscription still on one of the pillars of the court. The fountain in the center of the court, however, was restored by the Sultan Housam el-Din Lagin, in A.D. 1296. The minaret is characteristic of the eclectic taste of Housam; although its plan and elevation are unique, certain details of the decorative motifs of the masonry correspond to those found in mosques thousands of miles apart. Following examples from mosques in Spain at Seville and Cordova, the arches of this arcade around one of the courtyards of the Tulun mosque are supported on tiers of brick in the corners of which are little columns.

EL-AZHAR MOSQUE. *Shi'ite Fatimid Caliphate.* *p. 17*

The mosque of El-Azhar, called "The Sumptuous," was named after Fatima ez-Zahra, the daughter of the Prophet Mohammed, and built to serve the Fatimid Dynasty. Although founded about A.D. 970, the present mosque is an amalgam of various building periods. Each successive generation, nevertheless, respected the earlier styles, reflecting a conscious attempt to blend additions into the existing structures. The porticoes are supported by three hundred columns whose marble was appropriated from various buildings erected during Egypt's Greek and Roman Periods. The light, delicate effect of this arcade contrasts with the heavy, ornamental quality of the two minarets, which date from the Mamluk Period. In A.D. 988, the Caliph El-Aziz founded a college at the mosque for the instruction of the Shi'ite sect of Islam; philosophy, chemistry and astronomy were added to the curriculum in A.D. 1005 by the Caliph El-Hakin.

THE BLUE MOSQUE. *Ayyubid Caliphate.* *p. 19*

Founded in A.D. 1346, the so-called "Blue Mosque" was restored in A.D. 1651 by an Ottoman officer called Ibrahim Agha Mustafizan, who is buried there. To Ibrahim can be attributed the interior decoration after which the mosque is named. The east wall is adorned with tiles of Persian faience comprising green and blue flowers on a white ground. The motifs in the figural panel to the left of the pulpit consist of plants and flowers in a vase along the central axis, flanked on each side by stylized representations of cypress trees. The use of tiles to decorate the interior of a mosque in Cairo dates from their introduction in this mosque.

THE "BLUE MOSQUE"
1346 A. D.
Cairo.
Ayyubid Caliphate.

THE GREAT PYRAMIDS. *Dynasty IV.*

In this view of the Giza plateau looking north, the pyramid built for the Pharaoh Cheops stands at extreme right. In its original state it rose 481 feet high and is estimated to have contained 2,300,000 blocks of stone averaging 2.5 tons each. In the center is the pyramid of his son Chephren, built on a rise so that it appears here to be taller; it is actually ten feet shorter. To the far left is the pyramid of Mycerinus, fronted by two of three small subsidiary pyramids which were never completed; the largest of these is believed to have been intended for the tomb of Mycerinus' queen, Khamerernebty II.

Despite pseudo-scientific speculation to the contrary, the pyramids at Giza are simply tombs—the final resting places of three of Egypt's Dynasty IV pharaohs. Although we lack contemporary written evidence describing how they were built, the account preserved in Book 2 of the *History* of Herodotus, who visited Egypt in the fifth century B.C., is fairly reliable. He recounts how gangs of 100,000 workmen, rotating in shifts of three months each, toiled for twenty years building the Great Pyramid of Cheops. This account agrees with what Egyptologists have learned. Egypt was a predominantly agrarian society with a polytheistic religion which included the divine pharaoh, and to labor for the pharaoh was tantamount to serving a god. But in the *Westcar Papyrus*—written during the Middle Kingdom—Cheops is depicted as a tyrant, whom the magician Djedi upbraids for the sadistic delight he took in mistreating people.

THE GREAT PYRAMIDS
Giza.
Dynasty IV (2600–2490 B.C.)

THE SOLAR BOAT. *Dynasty IV.*

In order to facilitate the passage of visitors around the Great Pyramid, the Egyptian Antiquities Department in 1951 decided to build a road along its south side. The construction was impeded by huge mounds of sand and rubble, the careful removal of which consumed almost four years before the ancient surface of the Giza plateau was reached. The excavators were then astonished to find that the southern wall of the Pyramid's precinct was 16½ feet closer to the base of the monument than they had calculated. The archaeologists, led by Kamal El Mallakh, uncovered a thick layer of composite ground—limestone powder, scraps of wood and charcoal—spread over a thick layer of mortar which held 41 limestone blocks in place, serving as the ceiling for a pit below. Here they discovered the funerary boat of Cheops, carefully dismantled with its component parts stacked in 13 orderly layers. The wood was as fresh as if it had been buried the year before. Then followed the painstaking work of reassembling the 1,224 pieces of wood of which it was made, ranging in length from 75 feet to less than 4 inches. Built of cedar imported from Lebanon and local Egyptian sycamore, the boat measures 139 feet and its total displacement is 150 tons. When first discovered, it was believed to be the solar barque of Cheops, which equated the deceased pharaoh with the Sun-God Re. Recent study, however, suggests that it constituted the funerary barque used by the priests in the funerary rites for Cheops to make pilgrimages from one site to another.

Pp. 22–23
THE SPHINX
Giza.
Reign of Pharaoh Chephren.
Dynasty IV (2510–2485 B.C.)

THE SOLAR BOAT
Giza.
End of reign of Cheops.
Dynasty IV (2550–2520 B.C.)

THE SPHINX. *Dynasty IV.*

pp. 22, 23

The builders of the Cheops Pyramid used the plateau at Giza as a quarry for that structure's inner core. When their work was ended, the quarrymen had inadvertently created a rocky hillock. During the following reign, the sculptors transformed that knoll into a sphinx, a composite beast which, in Egyptian art, combines the head of a reigning monarch with the body of a lion. The resulting figure, 240 feet long and 66 feet high, represents the Pharaoh Chephren wearing the royal *nemes* headdress with the *uraeus* attached, and the now missing false beard.

In Egyptian mythology, the sphinx, a vengeful but just deity who habitually vanquished enemies and symbolized the triumph of good over evil, was often placed before temples as a guardian. An extension of this role was afforded the Great Sphinx by the Egyptians of the New Kingdom, who regarded the sculpture as a representation of the God Harmakhis, "Horus of the Two Horizons." This solar deity was associated with the Gates of the Hereafter through which certain stars rose and set.

THE STEP PYRAMID, SAQQARA. *Dynasty III.*

The history of the site of Saqqara is dependent upon that of Memphis, for which it served as a cemetery. Occupying an area almost five miles in length and over a mile in width at its greatest expanse, Saqqara is the largest necropolis in all of Egypt, and the one in which traces of all important epochs of Egypt's long and distinguished history can be found. Its earliest monuments are the cenotaphs of the kings of Dynasty I, whose actual tombs were built

THE STEP PYRAMID
Saqqara.
Reign of Pharaoh Djoser.
Dynasty III (2620–2600 B.C.)

**TOMB CHAMBER,
PYRAMID OF KING UNAS**
Saqqara.
Dynasty V (2310–2290 B.C.)
The hieroglyphic inscriptions, which here comprise the so-called Pyramid Texts, are divided into 759 Spells, with many mythological allusions fundamental to our knowledge of Egyptian funerary rites.

at Abydos in Upper Egypt. During Dynasty III, the Step Pyramid was built by Imhotep for King Djoser, and some of the kings of Dynasty V and VI returned to Saqqara to build their pyramids, while during these same two dynasties many nobles built tombs at Saqqara which are remarkable for their scenes of daily life crisply carved in limestone and brilliantly painted.

PYRAMID OF KING UNAS. *Dynasty V.*
To the southwest of the Step Pyramid lies the Pyramid of King Unas (2310–2290 B.C.). In its interior are several chambers, including the TOMB CHAMBER proper (*above*), with the plundered granite sarcophagus of the king still standing. The glory of this pyramid is the decoration of the Central and Tomb Chambers, with their painted ceilings decorated with row after row of five-pointed stars in imitation of the vault of heaven. The walls are covered with hieroglyphic inscriptions cut into the stone and filled with blue pigment. These are collectively known as the *Pyramid Texts* and constitute the oldest collection of religious and funerary literature to survive from ancient Egypt.

TOMB OF NOFER. *Dynasty V.* *Left*

In an attempt to remain as close to their sovereigns as possible in the After-life, many of the nobles of Dynasty V and VI constructed their tombs at Saqqara in the vicinity of the pyramids of their kings. These tombs, called mastabas, are brilliantly decorated with painted reliefs. These had a symbolic function wherein, through sympathetic magic, the depiction of an object might become a reality. They are optimistic expressions of the joy of life and its concomitant activities, often recorded in minute detail. In the Tomb of Nofer, just south of the Pyramid of Unas, the wall at the left in this illustration is divided into five registers, which organizes the space and the ground lines upon which the action takes place. The lower register contains a mock river battle between teams of boatsmen.

Left
TOMB OF NOFER
Saqqara.
Late Dynasty V (2310–2290 B.C.)

**MASTABA OF MERERU-KA,
SACRIFICIAL CHAMBER**
Saqqara.
Early Dynasty VI (2290–2150 B.C.)

MERERU-KA IN STRIDING ATTITUDE
Tomb of Mereru-ka,
Saqqara.
Early Dynasty VI (2290–2150 B.C.)
The Scepter held by Mereru-ka in his lowered hand passes behind his body, in accordance with conventions of representation. His name and titles are contained in the columns of hieroglyphs over his head.

MASTABA OF MERERU-KA. *Dynasty VI.* *pp. 27, 28*

Among the largest at Saqqara, the Tomb of Mereru-ka, built at the beginning of Dynasty VI, contains thirty-one rooms and passages and, like that of Nofer, is decorated with scenes of daily life. The view reproduced here is of the north wall of the SACRIFICIAL CHAMBER (*p. 27*), whose ceiling is supported by six rock-cut pillars each of whose sides is decorated with striding representations of Mereru-ka himself. At the top of the small flight of steps is a stone table upon which offerings were made. Mereru-ka, in the guise of his statue, could therefore eternally partake of the offerings presented to him. The depiction of MERERU-KA IN STRIDING ATTITUDE (*p. 28*) in bold, raised relief on the pier of the Sacrificial Chamber is a typical example of the Egyptian artist's rendering of the human body in two dimensions. Both legs are shown in profile, the torso has been rotated so that it appears in front view, and the head is again shown in profile. The eyes, however, are in front view.

THE STEP PYRAMID, SAQQARA. *Dynasty III.* *Below*

Of all the monuments at Saqqara, none is more interesting for its architectural plan and design than the Step Pyramid. It was constructed under the direction of the Vizier Imhotep, whose genius was such that later generations

THE STEP PYRAMID
Saqqara.
Reign of King Djoser.
Dynasty III (2620–2600 B.C.)

IHY, THE OVERSEER OF LINEN,
MASTABA OF PTAH-HOTEP
Painted raised relief,
Saqqara.
Dynasty V (2450–2290 B.C.)

of Egyptians were to deify him. His renown sometimes eclipses that of his sovereign, the Pharaoh Djoser, for whom the monument was built. Until Dynasty III, the traditional form of a royal tomb was a mastaba. In fact, the Step Pyramid was originally conceived as such. At some stage the plans were altered and the pyramid grew as a series of six mastaba-like structures of progressively diminishing size placed one above the other, each recessed $6\frac{1}{2}$ feet from the outer edge of the lower one. The total height of the pyramid is 200 feet, and its ground plan is a rectangle measuring 413 by 344 feet.

Imhotep's most important accomplishment lies not so much in the final appearance of the structure as in the fact that it is made of stone. Heretofore, mudbrick had been the exclusive building material for royal mastabas. Imhotep, apprenticed in the mudbrick tradition, translated that medium into stone. The scope of his task was enormous when one considers that he commissioned the quarrymen to cut blocks of stone into the size and shape of the mudbricks they had been accustomed to use. The Step Pyramid at Saqqara was the first monumental architectural ensemble in all of ancient Egypt to employ stone as its exclusive material.

But the Step Pyramid is but one element of the Pharaoh Djoser's funerary complex. The area was wreathed with an enclosure wall 1,470 feet long by 885 feet wide. Part of this wall, at the entrance to the complex, has been reconstructed and is visible at the left in the illustration on page 29. Here again, Imhotep imitated mudbrick architecture which he translated into stone. The recessed panels with their tall, narrow niches are intended to break the monotony of a long, otherwise uninterrupted, wall, and by casting shadows increase the visual impact of the wall. Numerous subsidiary build-

30

HARVESTING SCENE,
MASTABA OF MERERU-KA
Painted raised relief,
Saqqara.
Dynasty V (2450–2290 B.C.)

ings used in the rites associated with the king are found within the enclosure wall. The Chapels of the Hebsed, or Jubilee Court are translations into stone of wattle and daub. Every detail of that primitive construction technique has been captured in stone, as if petrified. A careful study of these structures sheds much light on the architecture of the early dynasties of Egypt, whose buildings—all made of wattle and daub—are no longer extant for study.

PTAH-HOTEP MASTABA, SAQQARA. *Dynasty V.* *p. 30*
The Mastaba of Ptah-hotep at Saqqara contains what many contend are the most beautiful reliefs from the Old Kingdom in that necropolis. Built during Dynasty V by a man who held one of the highest offices of the state, the tomb celebrates the life and the daily activities of Ptah-hotep's estate. In this detail of one of the lower registers on the northern half of the west wall, IHY, THE OVERSEER OF LINEN (*p. 30*), is shown carrying two boxes suspended from a yoke, in which are seen various species of fowl caught in traps by his associates. The depiction exemplifies the Egyptians' interest in visual clarity, the fronts of the boxes being omitted so as to allow the spectator to see the birds within. The weight of the birds is indicated by the bend of the yoke. This reflection of gravity is countered by the spring in Ihy's stride, only his toes coming into contact with the ground line. The extraordinary detail in this figure cut in stone and colored, in which the receding hairline and the circumcision of Ihy are recorded, shows the careful observation of nature of the ancient Egyptians. In the field above the scene, the hieroglyphs are identifying captions with words or phrases associated with the action depicted, sometimes including vulgar colloquialisms.

31

HARVESTING SCENE, TOMB OF MERERU-KA.

Dynasty V.   *p. 31*

Agricultural scenes comprise a great proportion of ancient Egyptian tombs, since farming was one of the principal industries of the nation. In this detail from the Mereru-ka tomb, the two field workers harvesting the crop with sickles are joined by the central figure who appears to be accompanying their work with the sounds of a flute. A similar representation of a flautist amidst harvesters of flax is depicted in a mastaba now preserved in the Leiden Museum.

NUBIAN PRISONERS, TOMB OF HOREMHEB, SAQQARA.

Dynasty XVIII.

Although the royal tomb of Horemheb at Thebes had long been known, his tomb at Saqqara, constructed when he was a private citizen and Commander-in-Chief of the Army during the reign of Tutankhamun, outstrips the former in terms of opulence of carving and the consummate skill with which the scenes are depicted. Working within the established traditions and completely absorbed by the naturalism fostered by the religious reforms of Akhenaten, the artists employed at Saqqara by Horemheb pushed the limits of the Amarna style to new heights. Surpassing the reliefs of the Amarna period which prior to the unexpected discovery of this tomb in 1975 were considered a highwater mark, these reliefs are among the most sophisticated ever carved in ancient Egypt.

A group of seated Nubian captives, perhaps the result of one of Horemheb's

NUBIAN PRISONERS,
TOMB OF HOREMHEB
Sunk relief,
Saqqara.
Dynasty XVIII (1330–1305 B.C.)

EGYPTIAN SOLDIER LEADING A
CAPTIVE NUBIAN,
TOMB OF HOREMHEB
Sunk relief,
Saqqara.
Dynasty XVIII (1330–1305 B.C.)

campaigns, is found on the east wall of the second courtyard of the tomb. The
artist has rendered a crowd scene convincingly, with the squatting prisoners
bunched together. As a compositional device, two Nubians to the left of
center turn their heads backward to focus their attention in another direction.
Although all of these Southerners are shown wearing kilts and the same kind
of headdresses, each face is individualized and distinctive. One easily distin-
guishes their different ages ranging from maturity to old age by the lines
etched in the particular faces.

EGYPTIAN SOLDIER LEADING A CAPTIVE NUBIAN.
Dynasty XVIII.

A conflict of wills between the Nubian captive and his Egyptian escort is
captured with psychological insight in the expressive lines of this sunk relief:

33

the smaller Egyptian grasps the Nubian firmly by the forearm and raises his foot above the ground as he musters his strength to pull the man forward, while the Nubian appears to be doing his best to counter his captor's progress.

PAIR OF SCRIBES WRITING. *Dynasty XVIII.*

This detail of two scribes from the Horemheb tomb at Saqqara betrays a sensitivity of line and a feeling for plane rarely so harmoniously united. The distinctive profile of each face, the full, ever so gently parted lips, and the crease of the eyelids rendered by a faintly incised line all reveal the masterful skill of the stone cutter. Bent forward, both figures delicately poise their pens between thumb and index fingers. The far hands hold the palette whose top end is provided with two holes, one for red ink, the other for black, while the bottom is hollowed out to store extra reed pens. Although relying on overlapping planes to generate space, the body of the second scribe is almost completely concealed from view. Despite this compositional advance, the papyrus scrolls themselves are shown in top view, in accordance with the long-standing Egyptian tradition of simultaneity of views.

PAIR OF SCRIBES WRITING,
TOMB OF HOREMHEB
Sunk relief,
Saqqara.
34   *Dynasty XVIII (1330–1305 B.C.)*

II BENI HASAN, ABYDOS, DENDERA

BENI HASAN

During the Middle Kingdom the government of Egypt became decentralized. The position of the nobility eclipsed that of the pharaoh, particularly in the administration of local districts called nomes, and families of longstanding established regional dynasties of their own. As a result, the heads of these local districts, called nomarchs, did not feel the need to build their tombs next to those of their sovereign. In Middle Egypt, on the east bank of the Nile to the north of a desert ravine, the site of Beni Hasan contains approximately thirty-nine rock-cut tombs, mostly built during Dynasties XI and XII by the powerful nomarchs of this region. The stern entrance porticoes, with columns that anticipate Greek protodoric columns by a millennium and a half, belie lavishly decorated interiors. This dichotomy between exterior and interior reflects the sumptuary laws of the day which proscribed ostentatious displays of wealth which might rival royal monuments.

ROCK-CUT TOMBS OF BENI HASAN
Dynasties XI and XII (2100–1780 B.C.)

TOMB OF KHETY.   *Dynasty XI*   *Below*

The Tomb of Khety, nomarch of the Oryx Nome, consists of a single chamber with six columns cut from the living rock representing bound lotus stems with capitals in the form of buds. An inscription on the lintel requests a "good burial in the necropolis" for Khety. The rear wall is decorated with wrestlers in various positions in a lively style which exemplifies the Egyptian penchant for simultaneous movement, here giving the impression of cinematic stop action.

TOMB OF KHNUM-HOTEP III.   *Dynasty XII.*   *Right*

This tomb of the chief administrator of the Oryx Nome is more elaborate in plan, consisting of a porch and two interior chambers, the first of which is constructed with a tripartite vaulted ceiling. The major decoration of its east wall shows Khnum-hotep and his wife hunting in the marshes, one with a throw stick, the other harpooning fish. Over the door, Khnum-hotep is represented in the process of fowling with a trap. The top of the wall, where it joins the ceiling, is decorated with a *khekher* frieze, a motif used throughout Egyptian architecture to evoke, in a highly stylized manner, the walls of certain primeval sanctuaries constructed of pliant vines knotted together near their tops in wispy groups.

Left
TOMB OF KHETY
Beni Hasan.
Dynasty XI (2100–1990 B.C.)
Khety, nomarch of the Oryx Nome, was "Commander of the Troops in all the Difficult Places."

Right
TOMB OF KHNUM-HOTEP III
Beni Hasan.
Dynasty XII (1990–1780 B.C.)

ABYDOS.

The site of Abydos has a long and rich history. During the Archaic Period and the formative era of Dynasty I, when the foundations of Egyptian civilization were laid, Abydos served as the royal necropolis for the capital city of Memphis, whose monarchs also constructed cenotaphs at Saqqara (see pp. 25ff). As the political axis of Egypt changed and her monarchs selected other sites for their tombs and other cities for their capitals, Abydos gradually lost its royal character but emerged as one of the most important religious centers of the land. This emergence was the direct result of a characteristically Egyptian religious phenomenon of assimilation. In the beginning, a rather obscure local god, known only by the epithet of Khenti-amentiu, "Pre-eminent-among-the-Westerners," was the titular deity of the region. The god was depicted in canine form, and this probably represents an early attempt to transform a scavenger of burials into a protector of the deceased. Such transformations are not uncommon among primitive peoples. The destructive forces of the animal were thereby nullified and the care of "Westerners"— a euphemism for the deceased—was entrusted to this newly created deity. The fortunes of Khenti-amentiu became inextricably linked to those of the geographic area in which he was primarily worshiped. But as the site of Abydos waned, so did the importance of its primeval titular deity. This demotion may have been assisted by the spectacular rise of the cult of Osiris, the pre-eminent Egyptian god of the Hereafter. Of all the legends associated with him, none is more important for the re-establishment of Abydos as a religious center than that of his dismemberment. It is one of the ironies of

Right
SECOND HYPOSTYLE,
TEMPLE OF SETY I
Abydos.
Dynasty XIX (1305–1290 B.C.)

TEMPLE OF SETY I
Abydos.
Dynasty XIX (1305–1290 B.C.)

our knowledge of ancient Egypt that this legend is not preserved for us in an Egyptian account. We have to rely on Plutarch, a Roman who lived between A.D. 46–120. Plutarch, a priest for life of the Greek oracular God Apollo at Delphi, was interested in religious questions and his personal, mystical approach to religion is best evidenced by his *De Iside et Osiride*, written late in life. From that book one learns that after a series of outrages committed against Osiris by his archrival Seth, symbolizing the typhonic forces of evil, the body of Osiris is dismembered. Seth then scatters its fourteen parts hither and yon. Isis, the faithful consort of Osiris, succeeds in collecting the pieces, each of which she buries, and thereby founds a series of shrines to Osiris throughout Egypt, reminiscent of those built around reliquaries of saints in the Middle Ages of Europe. The head of Osiris was found at Abydos and interred there. Osiris, the new god of the deceased, assumed the attributes of Khenti-amentiu, so much so that one of the epithets of Osiris, now called "Lord of Abydos," is in fact "Pre-eminent-among-the-Westerners," the very name of Khenti-amentiu! The exact date of the assimilation of Khenti-amentiu with Osiris is problematic, but the process was completed by the Middle Kingdom.

TEMPLE OF SETY I, ABYDOS. *Dynasty XIX.* *pp. 38, 39*

The famous temple built by Sety I and completed and enlarged by his son Rameses II, is one of the best preserved of Dynasty XIX structures. In its architectural plan, its sanctuary is almost unique, having seven chapels rather

RAMESES II AND HIS SON LASSOOING A BULL
Sunk relief.
Passage off the South Wing, Temple of Sety I, Abydos.
Dynasty XIX (1290–1220 B.C.)

than one, each dedicated to a separate deity. Behind the second columned hall are rectangular shrines to Horus, Isis, Osiris, Amun, Hor-akhte, Ptah, and the deified King Sety. Atypical also is the complex of ancillary structures grouped in a wing which is entered by a long narrow gallery. On the right wall of this gallery is carved the celebrated List of Kings which begins with Menes, the traditional first king of Dynasty I, and ends with that of Sety himself. The lotus-bud columns of the SECOND HYPOSTYLE OF THE TEMPLE OF SETY I (*p. 39*), which are a modified form of the lotus plant columns in the Tomb of Khety (p. 36), contrast sharply with the stark angularity of the piers facing the now destroyed first two courts (p. 38). Thirty-six of these columns support the roof, their somewhat squat proportions being typical of some of the architectural forms of Dynasty XIX.

RAMESES II AND HIS SON LASSOOING A BULL.
Dynasty XIX   *p. 40*
The king, wearing the Red Crown of Lower Egypt, is shown capturing a wild bull with a rope. The rope has caught the bull by his horns and has ensnared a hind leg, effectively hobbling the beast, who struggles to escape. The king's son, identified by the side-lock of youth, seizes the bull's tail to curb its gait in an attempt to help his father. The position of hooves and feet relative to the ground line imparts a sense of liveliness to the scene. This wall decoration, in a passage off the Gallery of the List of Kings, is executed in sunk relief and the effect is entirely dependent on line.

OSIRIS ENTHRONED
Raised relief.
North wall of the Hypostyle Hall,
Temple of Sety I,
Abydos.
Dynasty XIX (1305–1290 B.C.)

OSIRIS, LORD OF ABYDOS, ENTHRONED.

Dynasty XIX. *p. 41*

On the north wall of the Hypostyle Hall, this superb relief depicts Osiris wearing the *atef* crown with ram's horns and the sun disc of the God Re. Osiris is seated on a throne on the side of which is carved the symbol of the union of Upper and Lower Egypt and on its lower edge the insignias of eternal life. Behind him stands his consort the Goddess Isis carrying the ritualistic throne on her head. Facing Osiris are the goddesses of Truth and Years, Maat and Renpet. Executed in the highly refined Amarna style of the previous dynasty, the delicate modeling of the facial features and the folds of skin on the throats are characteristic of Abydene reliefs.

BARQUE OF OSIRIS. *Dynasty XIX.* *Below*

On the north wall of the Chapel of Osiris, the god's sacred barque is shown resting on carrying poles which extend beyond the sides of the repository stone on which the vessel actually rests. On the deck, in the center, stands the baldachin enclosing the cult image of the god. The subsidiary figures are most probably gilded bronze statuettes which decorated the actual barque. The Nile being the principal highway of ancient Egypt, it was only natural for its gods to travel by boat.

BARQUE OF OSIRIS
Painted relief.
Shrine of Osiris, north wall,
Temple of Sety I, Abydos.
Dynasty XIX (1305–1290 B.C.)

Right
DEIFICATION OF SETY I
Painted relief.
Shrine of Sety I, west wall,
Temple of Sety I, Abydos.
Dynasty XIX (1305–1290 B.C.)

DEIFICATION OF SETY I. *Dynasty XIX.* *p. 43*

The inclusion of the shrine dedicated to Sety I among the seven sacred chapels in the temple of Abydos confirms his divinity. In keeping with this, the painted relief on the west wall of the shrine shows Sety in the guise of Osiris, attended not by priests but by other members of the Egyptian Pantheon. In the center the God Iuen-mut-ef, a manifestation of the deity Horus, offers incense to the Osirified Sety. At the left, his mother Isis, holding a sistrum, has here appropriated some of the attributes of the Goddess Hathor. On the east wall of the shrine is depicted SETY I GIVEN LIFE BY THE IBIS-HEADED GOD THOTH (*above*). The king, again in the raiment of Osiris, holds the flail and crook and wears the *atef* crown. Thoth, god of wisdom and writing, reaches the *ankh* sign of life toward the king's nostrils. The extensive use of overlapping, establishing spatial relationships between the figures, is a distinctive feature of this masterful relief.

TEMPLE OF HATHOR, DENDERA.

Ptolemaic Dynasty *Right*

44 The site of Dendera has a long and rich association with Hathor, its major

SETY I GIVEN LIFE BY THE IBIS-HEADED GOD THOTH
Painted relief, detail.
Shrine of Sety I, east wall,
Temple of Sety I, Abydos.
Dynasty XIX (1305–1290 B.C.)
The carving of this scene demonstrates the skill of Sety's craftsmen. In the overlapping of planes to establish depth, the flail held by Sety passes beneath his false beard and is fronted by the *ankh*, the sign of life, held by Thoth, whose outstretched arm in turn is overlapped by the two scepters in his other hand.

deity. As early as the Old Kingdom, the goddess was worshiped at this site, which was also the capital of the Sixth Nome of Upper Egypt. Associated with the sycamore tree and manifest as the Divine Cow who nursed pharaohs, Hathor was the flamboyant goddess of love and joy, and mistress of gold. There is little wonder, therefore, that the Greeks equated the Egyptian Hathor with their own goddess Aphrodite. Her temple at Dendera is the creation of the late Ptolemaic and early Roman periods. The tendency in the past has been to ascribe no qualitative values to Egyptian monuments produced during the Greek and Roman epochs. Such summary, prejudicial treatment is barely consonant with the lasting value such monuments hold for the scholar. The temple of Hathor at Dendera is no less magnificent than that of Sety I at Abydos. Although it lacks a colonnade and the two pylons which ought to precede the main sanctuary proper, the design of the facade is unique. The outline of the exterior wall, with its sloping sides and cavetto cornice, frames six columns in the shape of sistrums (the sacred rattles of the cult), each with the bovine head of Hathor. Six intercolumnar slabs, each with offering scenes, symmetrically flank the entrance to the Hypostyle Hall. The ceiling of the latter is decorated with astronomical figures, and the walls with rites associated with the foundation and dedication of a temple. The ceiling of a small kiosk which served as a shrine of Osiris contains a circular representation of the Zodiac as we know it, with each of its twelve signs fully represented, which is the only one of its kind known from ancient Egypt.

TEMPLE OF HATHOR
Dendera.
Ptolemaic and Roman Period.
(*Second century B.C.—First century A.D.*)
Cartouches of Roman emperors from Augustus
to Nero appear among the inscriptions
on the walls.

Left
PRECINCT OF THE TEMPLE OF
HATHOR
Dendera.
*Dynasty XXX to Roman Period
(380 B.C.–100 A.D.)*
From bottom left: Birth House of Nectanebo I,
the Coptic Church (late 5th century A.D.),
and Birth House of Roman Emperor Augustus.
(30 B.C.–14 A.D.)

Above
SACRED LAKE, TEMPLE OF HATHOR
Dendera.
*Dynasty XXX to Roman Period
(380 B.C.–100 A.D.)*
This stone-lined ceremonial basin is the best
preserved of its type in any Egyptian temple.
Remains of massive mudbrick enclosure wall in
background.

PRECINCT OF THE TEMPLE OF HATHOR, DENDERA.
Ptolemaic Dynasty

Egyptian temples were seldom constructed in isolation; they usually formed
one unit within a precinct shared by subsidiary buildings used in the cult.
Dendera was no exception, and the main sanctuary of Hathor was supple-
mented by ancillary structures, including the Mammisi (Birth House) and the
Sacred Lake. All these were enclosed within a wall of mudbrick erected
around the perimeter of the precinct to insulate the gods and their priests
from the outside world. The enclosure wall at Dendera is in a remarkably
good state of preservation, and is visible behind the three buildings including
the so-called Mammisi of Augustus (p. 46) and beyond, the SACRED LAKE
(*p. 47*). Broadly speaking, a Mammisi is a structure within which the mysteries associated with the birth of the titular deity's offspring, habitually a
child-god, were celebrated. At Dendera, Hathor and her consort Horus were
the parents of Ihy, also known as Harsomtous. To the God Ihy was dedicated
the best preserved of three structures in this area of the sanctuary, erected
during the reign of the Roman Emperor Augustus who added Egypt to his
realm by defeating Antony and Cleopatra. The ruins of an earlier Birth
House, begun by Pharaoh Nectanebo I of Dynasty XXX, and completed
under the early Ptolemies is seen at extreme left. Between the two Mammisis
are the remains of a Coptic church, built at the end of the fifth century A.D.,
and belonging to perhaps the second oldest Christian architectural complex
in Egypt. It is a three-nave basilica with a trilobe apse.

47

THE GOD BES. *First Century A.D.* *Right*

Among the divinities associated with the rites of the Divine Birth was the God Bes, ordinarily regarded as the protective spirit of childbirth, whom recent investigation has shown to be a late development of a native Egyptian priest in the guise of a lion. As in this high relief, Bes is usually represented with the head of a lion and the body of a dwarf. Of all the lesser divinities of the Egyptian pantheon, Bes was a staunch protector of those who invoked his aid. Consequently his image is frequently carved on beds and chairs, objects of daily use which come into direct contact with the human body.

ROMAN GATEWAY. *First Century A.D.* *Below*

Within the north side of the enclosure wall, along the north-south axis of the Temple of Hathor, lies the main entrance to the sanctuary, in the form of a monumental Gateway made of stone and decorated with reliefs. The present Gateway was built in the first century A.D. under the Roman Emperor Domitian, who had such deep interest in things Egyptian that he became involved with the sanctuary of Isis at Benevento in Italy, where an Egyptianized obelisk, inscribed with his titulary hieroglyphs, is still preserved. On the Gateway appear the cartouches of Trajan and Nerva; and a dromos, or processional road, led to it, flanked by an avenue of sphinxes, some of which are still preserved. The Gateway was kept locked, but on the major festivals of Hathor celebrated at Dendera, particularly the New Year's Festival, the doors were flung open for the faithful to enter.

THE GOD BES
Colored high relief.
First century A.D.
Temple of Hathor, Dendera.

ROMAN GATEWAY,
PRECINCT OF TEMPLE OF HATHOR
Dendera.
First century A.D.

III VALLEY OF THE KINGS

From earliest times the material wealth of Egyptian kings buried with their bodies in their tombs was destined to attract attempts to violate their eternal resting places. No tomb in Egypt was safe. As early as the Old Kingdom the original tomb of Queen Hetep-heres, wife of the Pharaoh Snofru and mother of Cheops, was plundered. The remains of that burial were piously exhumed and reinterred in a shaft near his own pyramid by her son Cheops. But the lure of a windfall was not the only motivation for such activities. The construction and decoration of a tomb was a tedious and necessarily costly undertaking. The Egyptians soon recognized the economics of usurping, or taking over as their own, earlier tombs by simply replacing the original owner's name with their own. Often, in such usurpations, the decorations remained virtually intact. Thus violating and usurping tombs became a not uncommon activity. This was particularly true for royal tombs, which were the results of state-directed efforts.

BURIAL CHAMBER
Tomb of Amenhotep II,
Valley of the Kings (No. 35).
Dynasty XVIII (1440–1410 B.C.)

THE ROYAL NECROPOLIS. *Dynasties XVIII-XX.*

In the sixteenth century B.C., at the beginning of Dynasty XVIII, Egyptian funerary architecture experienced a radical transformation. Since the time of mastaba tombs of the Archaic Period, the burial chamber containing the sarcophagus at the end of a deep shaft had virtually always been directly connected with the pyramid or sanctuary above ground to which it belonged. The innovation of the architects of the New Kingdom consisted in their treatment of the shaft as a separate, independent element.

In an effort to protect the body of the pharaoh in its sarcophagus chamber, the pioneering architects of the New Kingdom conceived the idea of isolating the actual tombs from the funerary temples and shrines devoted to the deceased. They selected a remote area of Western Thebes bounded by steep cliffs and practically inaccessible. This was to become the site of the royal burials for the kings of Dynasties XVIII to XX.

The concept of each tomb in the Valley is the same, consisting of passageways and chambers cut into the living rock, at the end of which was placed the sarcophagus. The tombs vary in length, some being 700 feet long and excavated to a depth in excess of 300 feet. Once cut, the individual tombs were then decorated with religious scenes. After the funerary rites were completed, and the king's body came to rest in the interior, the tomb was sealed. The hillside into which the tomb had been hewn was "restored" to its original appearance

ISIS KNEELING ON THE SIGN OF GOLD
Sarcophagus of Amenhotep II,
Tomb of Amenhotep II,
Valley of the Kings (No. 35).
Dynasty XVIII (1440–1410 B.C.)

51

by using the excavated rock to camouflage the exterior by re-creating the talus slope on the hillside. A special force was then entrusted with patrol duties to guard against intruders. The Valley is so isolated that even today, in the dead of night, the sounds of anyone moving along its slopes are distinctly audible. Having isolated the burial shaft and effectively attempted to protect it from plunder, the architects turned their attention to constructing the temples and ancillary structures associated with the cult and rites of the deceased king in the plains nearer the Nile, removed in space from the Valley. The evolution of funerary architecture had now reached its term; the closely integrated plan of the Old Kingdom pyramid field was now transformed into a series of architecturally independent structures, separated in space and only metaphysically united by the complexities of Egyptian religious thought. Yet despite these efforts at protection, the Royal Tombs in the Valley of the Kings were systematically looted in antiquity by the ancient Egyptians themselves. We have only to turn to surviving papyri to know how prevalent that was.

The Englishman Richard Pococke, the first modern traveler to leave an account of a visit to the Valley, described fourteen tombs seen by him in 1737; today, over sixty are known and these have been numbered in the order of their discovery, Number 1 assigned to that of Rameses VII, and Number 62 to that of Tutankhamun.

BURIAL CHAMBER, TOMB OF AMENHOTEP II.
Dynasty XVIII. *p. 50*

The king's body in the Tomb of Amenhotep II was discovered within a sarcophagus of quartzite, a material generally reserved for works of art of

SEVENTH HOUR OF THE AM DUAT
Tomb of Tuthmosis III,
Valley of the Kings (No. 34).
Dynasty XVIII (1490–1440 B.C.)

52

exceptional importance. The decoration is restrained and straightforward, with all secondary matter eliminated. By raising the ground line and utilizing large areas of empty, undecorated space, the artist achieved an elegant, balanced effect having strong visual appeal. Anubis, Guardian of the Dead, is represented once on each end of the side panels together with two of the four sons of Horus. At the head end is the Goddess Nephthys, while her counterpart, the goddess Isis, decorates the foot end. In the representation of ISIS KNEELING ON THE SIGN OF GOLD (*p. 51*), the divine wife of Osiris is shown leaning on the *shen* sign of eternal life. The elegant contour of her body and limbs is preserved in the strict silhouette profile view, behind which the other limbs are hidden. The two columns of inscriptions represent a spell addressed by Isis to Amenhotep which reads "to make bright his face and to open his eyes."

HOURS OF THE AM DUAT, TOMB OF TUTHMOSIS III.
Dynasty XVIII.   *pp. 52–53*

The charms and spells needed to protect the soul of the deceased on his voyage in the Netherworld form the decorations in several of the chambers of the Tomb of Tuthmosis III, whose mighty military campaigns abroad and their resulting conquests laid the foundations of the Egyptian Empire in the East. In this tomb, the stick figures in black lines on a buff ground evoke the calligraphy of certain religious papyri. All of these scenes belong to a liturgical treatise commonly known as the *Am Duat*, "The Book of That Which is

TWELFTH HOUR OF THE AM DUAT
Tomb of Tuthmosis III,
Valley of the Kings (No. 34).
Dynasty XVIII (1490–1440 B.C.)

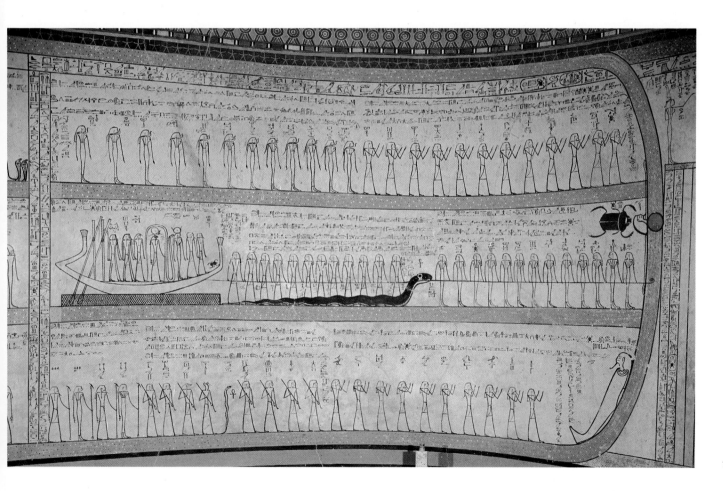

in the Netherworld." This work is a synthesis of acute astronomical observation and religious speculation. For the ancient Egyptians, the sun seen setting in the western horizon only to reappear in the east the following morning represented the quintessential symbol of resurrection. By analogy, the king, if likened to the sun, could die only to be revived in the Hereafter. The issue to be resolved was the route taken by the sun in its nocturnal journey; and to explain this, those early mythographers—the priests— proceeded from the scientific to the speculative. They used the roofs of their temples as observatories from which to map the heavens, paying particular attention to the stars. Using a simple plumb and the *merkhet*—a slotted stick which could be called an ancestor of the seaman's sextant—two priests could plot the movement of the hour stars. Several examples of star diagrams, ostensibly based on these observations, have survived. After repeated sightings, the collected data was studied and formed the basis for postulating a 24-hour day, twelve hours of which were reserved for the sun's nocturnal journey. The Egyptians believed that, since the darkness harbored Evil, the sun was beset by dangers threatening its reappearance. These dangers could be conveniently grouped into twelve categories, or hours. The *Am Duat*,

THE GODDESS ISIS, detail
Well Room, southwest wall,
Tomb of Horemheb,
Valley of the Kings (No. 57).
Dynasty XVIII (1330–1305 B.C.)

54

then, was a religious handbook, divided into hours, intended to provide the spells and charms necessary to nullify the forces of darkness during the twelve-hour nocturnal journey to the Hereafter.

In the SEVENTH HOUR OF THE AM DUAT (*p. 52*), the first register contains a series of divinities many of whom remain anonymous—making it difficult to interpret the precise significance. At the left is a seated god holding a knife, preceded by a leonine-headed goddess and a human-headed cobra. An exceptionally long serpent arches its body to form a shrine over the enthroned deity wearing a crown with double plumes. These are the protector deities of the entourage of Osiris who are invoked to protect the king, as the sun god, from his enemies—some of whom are represented beheaded to the right of center while others, further on, are lying on the ground, overpowered by a deity who holds them in check with a lock of hair. In like fashion, the king will vanquish his foes and will continue on his journey through the Netherworld. The lower register of the Seventh Hour represents the solar barque which transports the sun-god, shown standing in the center as a ram-headed male figure. The coil of a serpent, named the Enveloper, forms a deck cabin over him. On the deck stands a crew of eight, five of whom are standing

HOREMHEB IN THE COMPANY OF THE GODS
Well Room, east wall,
Tomb of Horemheb,
Valley of the Kings (No. 57).
Dynasty XVIII (1330–1305 B.C.)

HOREMHEB FACING HARSIESE
AND HATHOR
Well Room, east wall,
Tomb of Horemheb,
Valley of the Kings (No. 57).
Dynasty XVIII (1330–1305 B.C.)

57

abreast in groups of three and two respectively. Careful examination reveals how the scribe rendered these groups. The Goddess Isis stands on the prow and pronounces the incantations necessary to speed the solar barque along its way. To the right, the forces of Evil, personified as a serpent, are rendered harmless by a goddess and god who bind the snake which has already been transfixed with knives.

In the TWELFTH AND FINAL HOUR OF THE AM DUAT (*p. 53*), twelve goddesses with serpents resting on their shoulders stand behind twelve gods, all of whom raise their arms in adoration, anticipating the rebirth of the king at dawn. The second register again represents the solar barque with its crew, this time towed by twelve gods and thirteen goddesses. The center is occupied by a large black serpent named "Life of the Gods." The twenty-five towing deities enable the solar barque to be pulled into the tail, along the backbone, and out of the mouth of the serpent. The Egyptians, uncertain of the exact nature of the paths of the sun to be traveled during the nocturnal journey, formulated a considerable number of metaphors in their attempt to

Above
OSIRIS ENTHRONED ATTENDED BY ANUBIS, detail
Well Room, north wall,
Tomb of Horemheb,
Valley of the Kings (No. 57).
Dynasty XVIII (1330–1305 B.C.)

THE GOD HARSIESE, detail
Well Room, east wall,
Tomb of Horemheb,
Valley of the Kings (No. 57).
Dynasty XVIII (1330–1305 B.C.)

provide for any contingency. The lowest register represents two divine couples, four deities with oars, one of whom is serpent-headed while another has two heads of birds, a divine serpent standing on its tail, four deities with oars, and ten more standing in adoration. The metaphor is complete. The mummy of the king, shown at the extreme right of the lowest register and labeled "Image of Flesh," has been saved. The king, as the sun god in the form of the sacred scarab, is emerging like the sun at dawn at the right end of the central register.

TOMB OF HOREMHEB, VALLEY OF THE KINGS.
Dynasty XVIII.   *pp. 54–59*

Not all of the decoration in the tombs in the Valley of the Kings is devoted to such arcane religious subjects. More traditional representations of the king offering to readily identifiable members of the Egyptian pantheon are known. Many are outstanding aesthetic achievements and deserve close examination. Notable in this respect is the Tomb of Horemheb, last pharaoh of Dynasty XVIII. While still a commander of the army, Horemheb commissioned the

OSIRIS ENTHRONED, ATTENDED BY
ANUBIS AND HARSIESE
Well Room, north wall,
Tomb of Horemheb,
Valley of the Kings (No. 57).
Dynasty XVIII (1330–1305 B.C.)

P.61
OFFERING SCENE
Sarcophagus Chamber C,
Tomb of Rameses I,
Valley of the Kings (No. 16).
Dynasty XIX (1305–1300 B.C.)

59

construction of a tomb at Saqqara which just recently has been rediscovered (*pp. 32–34*). Taking advantage of the political circumstances surrounding him, Horemheb was installed as pharaoh and commissioned a second tomb, appropriate to his new station, in the Valley of the Kings. This tomb contains its share of religious scenes depicting the *Am Duat*, but the more traditional figural representations are arresting. One is immediately struck by the blue background which acts as a foil against which the brilliantly colored figures emerge and which may have been intended to represent the Hereafter. The scenes are harmoniously arranged along the walls in strict symmetry, as seen in the southern part of the east wall in the so-called Well Room, with the central axis prominently reserved for the representation of HOREMHEB IN THE COMPANY OF THE GODS (*p. 55*). The detail of the GODDESS ISIS from the southwest wall (*p. 54*) reveals a masterful execution. The prominent nostrils and delicate lines of flesh at the base of the throat in this spellbinding reprentation of the goddess provided a model for the artists working for Sety I. Sety's artists were no mere imitators but heightened Horemheb's style by the addition of more subtle modeling of facial features, torso and limbs. A comparison between the detail of HATHOR, IN THE TOMB OF SETY I (*p. 62*), and that of Hathor, the leftmost figure in the east wall of the Well Room in the tomb of Horemheb, representing HOREMHEB FACING HARSIESE AND HATHOR (*p. 56*) is instructive. The Ramesside example is more elaborate not only in the detail lavished on the wig and earring but also in the execution of the physiognomy of the goddess. The difference between the tombs of Horemheb at Saqqara and Thebes is a watershed between two styles. His Memphite tomb (pp. 32–33) represents the final chapter of the luxuriant naturalism of Amarnan art. His Theban tomb (pp. 54–59) anticipates the refined, courtly style of the last flowering of the Egyptian empire under the Ramesside pharaohs.

OFFERING SCENE, TOMB OF RAMESES I.
Dynasty XIX.   *Right*
The extent to which the artists employed for Rameses I, founder of Dynasty XIX, attempted to imitate the decoration in the tomb of his immediate predecessor, Horemheb, is clearly demonstrated in this offering scene. The dependence of one tomb on the other may reflect the special relationship between Rameses I and Horemheb. Rameses' father was a captain of troops under Horemheb, who as pharaoh appointed the son to the position of vizier of Egypt—which enabled the latter eventually to become king. The wall of the offering scene of which this is a detail maintains the blue background and brilliant color found in Horemheb's tomb; but the figural style is weaker. The king, in the center, is shown squatting between personifications of the primeval spirits of the cities of Pe and Nekhen, represented as a hawk-headed and a jackal-headed deity respectively. It is a scene of jubilation, in which the figures, striking their chests with alternating blows of their palms, represent an ancient ritual celebrating the rejuvenation of the *ba*, or soul, of the king.

TOMB OF SETY I, VALLEY OF THE KINGS.
Dynasty XIX.   *pp. 62–64*
The Tomb of Sety I, one of the most impressive hypogea in the Valley of the Kings, was long nicknamed "Belzoni's Tomb," in honor of the Italian explorer and draughtsman who discovered it in October 1817. Over 320 feet in length, and comprising over ten major chambers and passageways, its relief

THE GODDESS HATHOR, detail
Right wall of Second Lesser Chamber,
Tomb of Sety I,
Valley of the Kings (No. 17).
Dynasty XIX (1305–1290 B.C.)

KING SETY I, detail
Right wall of Second Lesser Chamber,
Tomb of Sety I,
Valley of the Kings (No. 17).
Dynasty XIX (1305–1290 B.C.)

sculptures represent a culminating point in the art of the Valley, rivaling that found in the Temple of Sety at Abydos (pp. 42–44). The subtlety of line and even of stately characterization in the detail of SETY I (*p. 62*), from the scene of the king with his arms at his side confronting Horus, demonstrates the high level of technical execution in Ramesside art, in which unfortunately the color here has been lost. On the same wall, the representation of the GODDESS HATHOR (*p. 62*) is one of the more elaborate in the tomb. The inscription identifies her as "Hathor, the Headmistress of Thebes, Lady of Heaven, Mistress of all the Gods." In keeping with her function as the goddess of love and joy, she is shown being offered a jug of wine by Sety.

THE SUN'S JOURNEY. TOMB OF SETY I.
Dynasty XIX.   *Below*

As the spells became inextricably linked to the funerary decoration of the royal tombs at Thebes, more time was spent on their execution and the stick figure quality of the representations found in the tombs of Amenhotep II and Tuthmosis III was fleshed out. By the time of Dynasty XIX, elaborate care was lavished on similar representations, as indicated by the treatment on the right wall of the Hall of the Four Pillars in the Tomb of Sety I. The scene depicting one hour in the *Book of Gates* is a richer, more florid elaboration of the calligraphic treatment in the tombs of Dynasty XVIII discussed above. The result, to the modern eye, is a more comprehensible design which is visually pleasing. But the scenes lack the aura of the mysterious unknown which permeates the earlier representations.

THE SUN'S JOURNEY
Hall of the Four Pillars,
Tomb of Sety I,
Valley of the Kings (No. 17).
Dynasty XIX (1305–1290 B.C.)

63

THE NORTHERN CONSTELLATIONS, CEILING IN TOMB OF SETY I. *Dynasty XIX.* *Above*

The Egyptian conception of the constellations of the heavens differs markedly from our own. The modern zodiac is a direct descendant of that evolved by the Greeks, who adopted and modified the astronomical tenets of the ancient Mesopotamians. How the Egyptians visualized the constellations is shown in the ceiling decoration in the sarcophagus chamber behind the pillared hall in the Tomb of Sety I. Here, among representations of the decans, are depictions of the Northern Constellations, which correspond to our group containing the Big Dipper. For the Egyptians, the Big Dipper was invariably called *Mes* and associated with a bull. It was not until the New Kingdom, however, that the constellation was depicted as a bull striding on some as yet unidentifiable support and invariably facing away from the hippopotamus. The latter is always represented as a female in a standing posture, with her front paws resting on one or more mooring posts, and occasionally but not invariably shown with a crocodile riding on her back. The Bull and the Hippopotamus are always associated with the Northern Constellations and always represented. The other constellations vary in the way they are represented. The falcon-headed *An* appears at the legs of *Mes*, perpendicular to her body's axis. The seated lion, always placed above a second crocodile, habitually occupies the lower left-hand quadrant and invariably faces *Mes*. These visual conceptions, which may include one or more heavenly bodies from several of our constellations, cannot be equated one to one with those constellations. The identification of the Big Dipper with the Bull is certain, since the Egyptian conception has been preserved in the modern Arabic name for that constellation.

THE NORTHERN CONSTELLATIONS
Ceiling, Sarcophagus Chamber C,
Tomb of Sety I,
Valley of the Kings (No. 17).
Dynasty XIX (1305–1290 B.C.)

THIRD CHAPTER OF THE BOOK OF GATES, TOMB OF RAMESES I. *Dynasty XIX.* *Below*

Careful observation of the thirty-six decans—or divisions of the solar equator—enabled the Egyptians to evolve a day of twenty-four hours, twelve of which were allocated for the night. An entire mythology was evolved around these hours and the portals of the Netherworld through which the deceased was required to pass before his resurrection at dawn. The so-called *Book of Gates*, like the *Am Duat* and other funerary texts, was intended to explain the nature of the nocturnal journey in yet other terms and to equip the deceased with the knowledge necessary for the successful negotiation of that journey. The representation in Sarcophagus Chamber C of the Tomb of Rameses I represents one version of the Third Division, or Third Chapter, of the *Book of Gates*. Nine recumbent mummies—eight of whom are illustrated here in silhouette—are painted black to symbolize the eternal state of death. Each is named by his accompanying hieroglyphs above, in the field which is intended to represent his sepulchre. Collectively, these nine represent the gods in the entourage of Osiris. The central register is occupied by inscriptions dealing with this Division. The scene below is perhaps the most curious representation in the *Book of Gates*. Twelve goddesses, in two files of six, each symbolizing one of the twelve hours of the night, stand on a mystical depiction of the Netherworld in the form of a pair of right triangles. Each of these triangles is bisected into sections symbolizing water and land—the blue areas shaded by curvilinear lines indicating ripples and the black areas representing the land. On each triangle, three goddesses stand on water,

THIRD CHAPTER OF
THE BOOK OF GATES
Sarcophagus Chamber C,
Tomb of Rameses I,
Valley of the Kings (No. 16).
Dynasty XIX (1305–1300 B.C.)

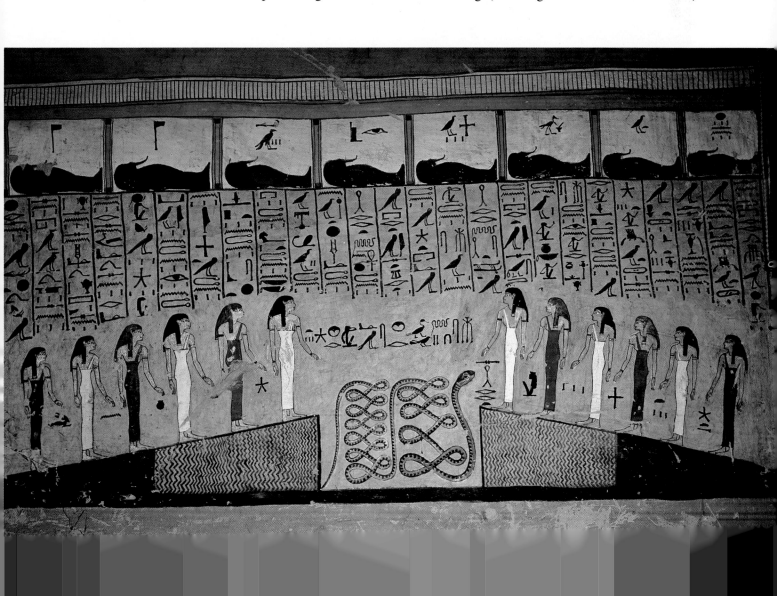

CEILING WITH SUN DISC
Corridor B,
Tomb of Merenptah,
Valley of the Kings (No. 8).
Dynasty XIX (1225–1210 B.C.)

three on land. In the area between lurks a serpent of many coils, designated as "He-who-should-be-removed." To avoid such monsters, the twelve-hour nocturnal journey over water and land had to be carefully undertaken in order to assure entrance into eternity.

KING IN THE COMPANY OF DEITIES.

Dynasty XVIII.   *pp. 66–67*

The less schematic mythological representations in some of the royal tombs of Dynasty XVIII would seem to indicate that the artists worked from pattern books or master copies, whose designs were modified to meet the spatial requirements of the tomb. Careful comparisons of mythological representations of the *Am Duat* or of *The Book of Gates* on the walls of tombs can often reveal the ability of the various artists and how successful their attempts at design were. Although it is difficult to illustrate complete walls of the purely religious texts in an attempt to demonstrate the quantitative differences which exist among them, a similar exercise can be performed for some of the more straightforward figural representations.

In the antechamber wall of the Tomb of Tuthmosis IV, the underlying principle of design consists of pairs of confronted figures, in each case depicting the king facing a protective divinity. Each representation of the king is similar with regard to costume, coloration and gesture. The same can be said for the figures of the deities, the goddesses being only distinguished from each other by the variations in the design on their respective dresses. One can easily imagine recourse to a pattern book from which the figures have been monotonously repeated on the wall. The figures themselves are too closely

Pp. 66–67
KING IN THE COMPANY OF DEITIES
Antechamber,
Tomb of Tuthmosis IV,
Valley of the Kings (No. 43).
Dynasty XVIII (1415–1405 B.C.)

ANUBIS GUARDING A TOMB;
ANUBIS ADMINISTERING THE
MUMMIFICATION RITUAL
Corridor E, left wall,
Tomb of Rameses III,
Valley of the Kings (No. 11).
Dynasty XX (1190–1160 B.C.)

spaced and an overall feeling of overcrowding prevails. The yellowish color of the background shares its tonality with the red-ochre flesh tones of the gods, the pale yellow of the goddesses, and the red of their dresses. This uniformity of tone contributes to a lack of vitality, despite the contrasting night sky ceiling of blue studded with gold stars.

In the hands of a more talented artist, the patterns discussed here could be made more visually arresting. Compare, for example, the paintings on the east wall of Horemheb's Theban tomb (pp. 56–57), where the representations of the king paired with a deity are based on the same tradition as that of Tuthmosis IV. Yet in each figure the details of costume and the gestures of the hands are varied, as are those of the gods and goddesses. The monotony of paired figures has been compositionally improved by omitting one figure of the king and creating a frieze of figures in which the representation of the king alternates with that of a deity. These departures from the basic pattern are enhanced and accentuated by the blue background, which visually detaches the figures from the plane of the wall. Particularly brilliant is the scene of OSIRIS ENTHRONED (*p. 59*), the god wearing the *atef* crown, and attended by the jackal-headed Anubis and falcon-headed Horus, on the north wall of the Well Room. The pure white of Osiris' mummy sheath and the highly symbolic terre-verte green of his face and hands stand out in sharp contrast against the sparkle of the hieroglyphs above and the ritualistic ornament on his throne.

LITANY OF THE SUN
Tomb of Rameses III,
Valley of the Kings (No. 11).
Dynasty XX (1190–1160 B.C.)

CEILING WITH SUN DISC, detail. TOMB OF MERENPTAH. *Dynasty XIX.*

p. 68

On the other hand, a predominantly yellow field succeeds in achieving a brilliant polychromatic effect in the ceiling of Corridor B in the Tomb of Merenptah, burial place of one of Rameses II's sons. A star-spangled night sky acts as a frame for the principal yellow field, of which the figural representation is confined to one end in this detail view. The rich red of the sun disc competes optically with the blue greens of the bird deity in its center. But the spectator's attention is gently drawn into the yellow field itself by the brown tonality of the feathers of the two birds symmetrically placed at the sides. The longer end of the spectrum is thus fully exploited by the integrated tonalities. The subject matter of this scene consists of the sun, personified as a ram-headed bird, protected by the Goddesses Isis at left, and Nephthys at right, in the form of kites standing on the shrines of the Two Horizons.

LITANY OF THE SUN, TOMB OF RAMESES III. *Dynasty XX.*

p. 69

The ancient Egyptians were pluralistic in formulating an iconography by which specific deities could be represented. As seen in the Tomb of Merenptah, the sun could be shown as a ram-headed bird. That shape was reserved for a particular aspect of this god whose forms could be extremely varied. In a decoration like the *Litany of the Sun*—which appears on the walls of several of the royal tombs of Dynasty XVIII and XIX and which, like the *Am Duat* and other religious compositions, attempted to explain the processes by which rebirth was effected—the sun-god appears in countless transformations. A detail of this prayer, as preserved in the Tomb of Rameses III, shows how varied those forms were and how complex those prayers. The different aspects of the sun-god, each accompanied by the appropriate spell, are here shown in a single file. The brightly colored forms against a white background and the use of varying amounts of empty space around the figures contribute to the isolation of each, thereby forcing the spectator's attention to rest on one image at a time. At the extreme right is the sun disc with the scarab Kheperi underneath, both of them symbols of the solar god. Four of the others are in human form, the others are either ram-headed or hawk-headed.

ANUBIS GUARDING A TOMB and ANUBIS ADMINISTERING THE MUMMIFICATION RITUAL. TOMB OF RAMESES III. *Dynasty XX.*

Right

Not all of the representations of the funerary rituals on the walls of the tombs of the pharaohs of the New Kingdom are as cryptic and arcane as those from the *Am Duat* of the *Book of Gates*. Some are quite graphically realistic. The left wall of Corridor E in the Tomb of Rameses III relies upon the iconography of the jackal-headed Anubis. In the upper register, Anubis lying on top of a mastaba is depicted in accordance with one of his traditional epithets as "He-who-is-upon-his-mountain." To the left and right are representations of Hapy and Kebeh-senu-ef, two of the four sons of Horus to whom the internal organs of the deceased were entrusted. The second register depicts Anubis, in the place of embalming, administering to the mummy of Rameses III, which lies on a lion-shaped bier, with the curving shape of the lion's tail rising in the field just behind Anubis. At the foot and head of the mummy kneel Isis and her sister Nephthys, protective goddesses of the deceased. The postures of both figures are identical to those found on the sarcophagus of King Amenhotep II (p. 51) and ultimately derive from the same model. The use of white serves as an exceptional background into which the brightly painted sunk relief is carved.

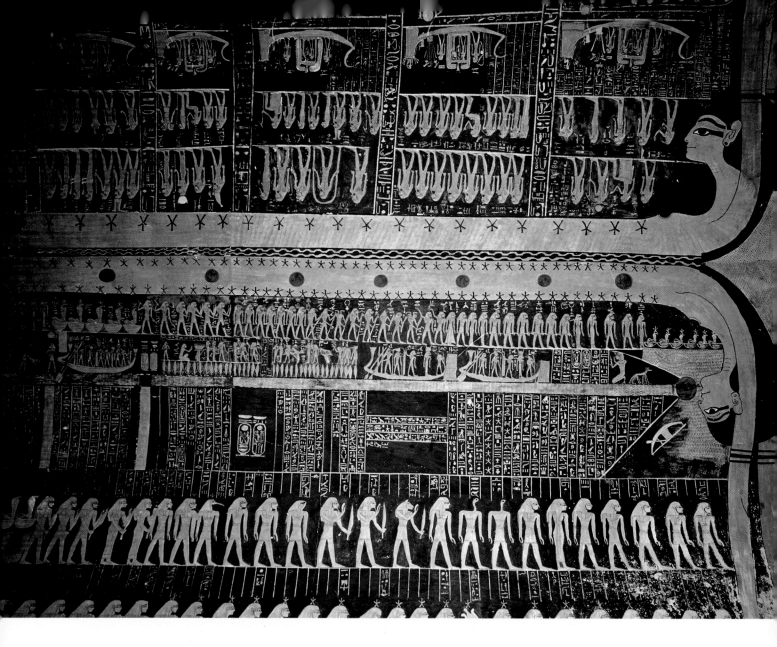

THE SKY GODDESS NUT. *Dynasty XX.*

This magical image decorating the ceiling of the Sarcophagus Hall of the Tomb of Rameses VI is based on depictions from the *Book of Day* and the *Book of Night*. These books were yet another attempt on the part of the Egyptian mythographers to explain the journey of the sun across the day and night sky. Its path is represented as passing along the body of the Sky Goddess Nut arching her head and torso over the earth, on which she supports herself with her arms and legs. At dawn, Nut gives birth to the sun which emerges from her loins and courses westward along her body until she swallows the heavenly body at sunset. The chapters of the *Book of Day* are represented in the lower half of this illustration, just as the *Book of Night* is represented in the upper half. During the night, the consumed sun courses within Nut only to emerge, reborn, at dawn. The metaphors are multilevel in these books, which also describe the diurnal journey as the course of the solar barque along the waters of the celestial river. The juxtaposition of these two images of Nut are not intended to represent her as twins. The characteristic convention of Egyptian simultaneity allowed for two distinct representations, one for the day, the other for the night, to avoid confusion.

THE SKY GODDESS NUT
Book of Day and Book of Night.
Ceiling, Tomb of Rameses VI,
Valley of the Kings (No. 9).
Dynasty XX (1150–1140 B.C.)

IV VALLEY OF THE QUEENS

TEMPLE OF HATHOR, DEIR EL-MEDINEH.
Dynasty XIX.

Just to the east of the Valley of the Queens lies the workmen's village and necropolis of the New Kingdom at Deir el-Medineh. The requirements of the inhabitants at Deir el-Medineh dictated the construction of numerous structures which, when taken together, provide a fairly complete picture of how an ancient Egyptian town of the New Kingdom functioned. This town was supplied with a succession of temples within a precinct which was continuously altered from Dynasty XVIII to the Ptolemaic Period. Within a mudbrick enclosure wall, built by the Ptolemies, is found the Sanctuary of Hathor, the celestial divine cow. Her cult here is analogous to that celebrated at Deir el-Bahari (p. 102). The small temple within the enclosure is of typical design, with slanting outer walls capped with a crowning cavetto cornice. The architectural elements of the doorway echo those of the building proper. Constructed during the reign of Rameses II, the outer walls are

TEMPLE OF HATHOR
Deir el-Medineh.
Dynasty XIX (1320–1200 B.C.)

undecorated. The stone temple is abutted on two sides by later constructions of mudbrick, several of which are visible in the view on page 73. The strong hold that Hathor had on the site is evidenced by the respect accorded this Ramesside temple by the Ptolemies who incorporated that structure into their rebuilding scheme at the site.

Pp. 74–75
TOMB OF NEFERTARI
OUTER HALL
Deir el-Medineh (No. 66).
Dynasty XIX (1290–1220 B.C.)

TOMB OF NEFERTARI. *Dynasty XIX.* *pp. 74–80*

Among the most beautifully decorated of all the Royal Tombs in Western Thebes, none can compare to the Tomb of Nefertari with its exquisitely painted reliefs, in the Valley of the Queens. Although Rameses II of Dynasty XIX had a large harem, Nefertari appears to have been his chief queen. She is represented as the sole celebrant in the cult of Hathor in the small or North Temple at Abu Simbel (p. 156) and here at Thebes was allowed her own tomb. This tomb was discovered in 1904 by the Italian Egyptologist Schiaparelli, in a small wadi in the southern sector of Western Thebes. Although used earlier for burials of lesser individuals, this area appears to have been selected for the exclusive use of queens and other members of the royal family at the beginning of Dynasty XIX. The earliest royal burial in this, the Valley of the

QUEEN NEFERTARI IN ADORATION, detail
Tomb of Nefertari,
Deir el-Medineh (No. 66).
Dynasty XIX (1290–1220 B.C.)

Queens, belongs to Satre, the queen of Rameses I, founder of the dynasty, and mother of Sety I.

The Tomb of Nefertari is arranged on an axial plan whose design is comparable to that of Sety I. It is cut into a limestone cliff which is of such poor quality that the architects deemed it necessary to cover the walls with a thick layer of plaster which, when dry, was sculpted. Consequently, the contours of the relief are bold and the details crisp. The resulting figural style, not dependent upon the vagaries of stone, is exceedingly harmonious throughout the tomb. The plaster enabled the sculptors to create scenes whose artistic expression is, in the opinion of some art historians, superior to that of the reliefs found in the Temple of Sety I at Abydos. These scenes are brilliantly painted in blazing colors which incorporate the whiteness of the plaster in the chromatic ensemble. This vibrant quality is further enhanced by the deep night-sky blue of the ceiling and the large, medial band of black serving as a kind of baseboard.

A view of the OUTER HALL into the southern part of the recess reveals the compositional concerns of the artists and their strict adherence to the axial

THE GODDESS ISIS
LEADING QUEEN NEFERTARI
Tomb of Nefertari,
Deir el-Medineh (No. 66).
Dynasty XIX (1290–1220 B.C.)

QUEEN NEFERTARI LED BY
THE GOD HARSIESE
Tomb of Nefertari,
Deir el-Medineh (No. 66).
Dynasty XIX (1290–1220 B.C.)

arrangement of the walls. The decoration of the lintel consists of a frieze of
alternating Cobras and Feathers of Truth, on each side of a kneeling god
each of whose outstretched hands rests on a circle containing an Eye of
Horus. The identification of the figure is debatable despite the fact that
vignettes accompanying Chapter 17 of *The Book of the Dead* are illustrated
with similar representations. This central figure assumes the same general
configuration as the vulture goddess with outspread wings on the lintel
behind. On the left and right walls are representations of Osiris and Anubis,
gods of the Netherworld. They are in their respective shrines, whose shapes
are different. The more traditional cavetto cornice crowns Anubis' shrine,
whereas Osiris, whose green face connotes floral regeneration, is shown in a
pavilion similar to that depicted in the scene in the Tomb of Sen-nedjem
(p. 130). The alternating of two distinct shrines and of an anthropomorphic
with a theriomorphic deity underlines the concern of the tomb's planners to
observe the laws of symmetry while allowing for variety in order to increase
the visual interest of the resulting composition.

The detail from QUEEN NEFERTARI IN ADORATION (*p. 76*) reveals the exceptionally fine modeling of the female figure in the thick plaster. The outspread fingers may be in the tradition of the late Amarna Period, while the repetition of two right hands is to be understood within the framework of Egyptian simultaneity. The festive gossamer dress is superbly rendered and produces a convincing illusion of a sheer negligee from which the forms of the body emerge. This interest is further exploited in the varying chromatic values used in the skin tones. There is a conscious attempt to model the face by shading the features with slightly differing tones of reddish-pink. This is particularly evident on the throat and cheeks. The lines on the neck, the prominent nostril, and the drilled corner of the mouth reflect the stylistic characteristics of the very best reliefs of the Temple of Sety I at Abydos.

THE GODDESS ISIS LEADING NEFERTARI.
Dynasty XIX. *p. 77.*
The elegance of the female form, with its slender, somewhat attenuated proportions, can be best appreciated in those scenes in which Nefertari appears in the company of deities. Led by Isis, who actually clasps the queen's hand, Nefertari is distinguished from the goddess in several ways. The facial features of Isis are smaller and more idealized than those of Nefertari whose broad nose and prominent chin imbue her with an individuality approaching portraiture. The queen's skin tones are those usually reserved for representations of males whereas the goddess is painted the yellow traditionally associated with female depictions. This chromatic difference optically cata-

SEVEN SACRED COWS AND BULL
Tomb of Nefertari,
Deir el-Medineh (No. 66).
Dynasty XIX (1290–1220 B.C.)

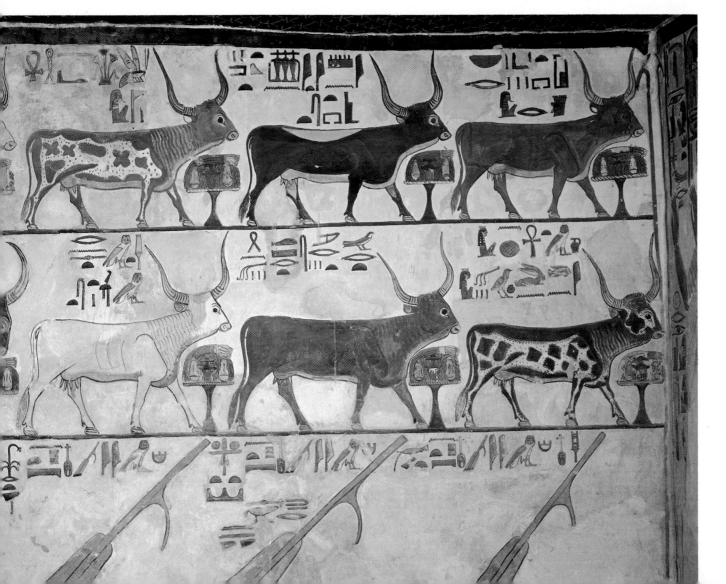

pults the representation of Nefertari to the fore and forces the spectator's eye to come to rest upon it. Scale has always been a factor in Egyptian scenes as a means of indicating importance. Nefertari, with her feathered headdress violating the borders of the black framing line, is slightly taller than Isis, and this imbues her with greater significance.

In the scene of NEFERTARI BEING LED BY THE HAWK-HEADED GOD HARSIESE (p. 78), the ideal of female beauty is nicely contrasted to that of the male. The queen's waist is higher emphasizing her thighs and elongated proportions. The simplicity of her costume contrasts sharply with the polychromed ensemble of the god to whose kilt is attached the ritualistic tail of a bull. The inscription above the queen presents her titulary, "The Great Queen, the Mistress of the Two Lands [Egypt], Nefertari, beloved of the Goddess Mut, the justified, the one revered under the Great God, Osiris."

NEFERTARI OFFERING LINEN TO THE GOD PTAH
Tomb of Nefertari,
Deir el-Medineh (No. 66).
Dynasty XIX (1290–1220 B.C.)

80

THE SEVEN SACRED COWS AND BULL.
Dynasty XIX. *p. 79*

The South Wall of the Side Room contains three registers of seven cows, one bull, and four oars whose tips are purposely omitted to give the impression of being dipped in the water. This unusual commingling of disparate elements is also found in Chapter 148 of *The Book of the Dead*. Despite its enigmatic nature, one assumes that the oars symbolize the powers of the gods which direct sustaining forces of the universe, as represented by the bovines. In front of each bovine is a table with offerings in the name of each: and the four rudders represent the cardinal points of heaven.

NEFERTARI OFFERING LINEN TO THE GOD PTAH.
Dynasty XIX. *p. 80*

Linen, so all-important in the embalming ritual, is proffered by Nefertari to the God Ptah, and is pictured in stylized fashion as four enlarged pieces of fringe. To the right, the God Ptah, described as the Lord of Truth, stands within a shrine. Behind him is a Djed Pillar, symbol of stability.

TOMB OF AMEN-HOR-KHEPESH-EF.
Dynasty XX. *pp. 81–84*

The same use of carved plaster and brightly painted relief is found in the Tomb of Amen-hor-khepesh-ef, a son of Rameses III of Dynasty XX. This

RAMESES III CLASPING HANDS WITH THE GOD IMSETY
Tomb of Amen-hor-khepesh-ef,
Valley of the Queens (No. 85).
Dynasty XX (1190–1160 B.C.)

tomb, also in the Valley of the Queens, was likewise discovered by Schiaparel-li, in 1904. Like that of Nefertari, the tomb was looted in antiquity. The scenes appear to be indebted to those found in the tomb of Nefertari but lack the variety found therein, which has been replaced by a strict, rigorous symmetry. The inscriptions themselves do not float in space but have been contained within yellow bands and placed so as not to interfere with the figures. The view into the SARCOPHAGUS CHAMBER (*p. 83*) reveals the balance of all the scenes. The damaged ceiling where the plaster has fallen away gives some idea of the thickness of the plaster coating and the technique by which the tomb was decorated. The relief, carved into the plaster, is carefully cut with great attention to detail and meticulously painted. An

RAMESES III CONFRONTING ISIS
Tomb of Amen-hor-khepesh-ef,
Valley of the Queens (No. 85).
Dynasty XX (1190–1160 B.C.)

Right
TOMB OF AMEN-HOR-KHEPESH-EF
Sarcophagus Chamber.
Valley of the Queens (No. 85).
Dynasty XX (1190–1160 B.C.)

examination of the costumes in the scene of RAMESES III CONFRONTING ISIS (*p. 82*) reveals these concerns. The proportions of the Goddess Isis recall those of Nefertari. The depiction of transparent garments, so noticeable in her tomb, is also in evidence here in the costume of the king's son—Prince Amen-hor-khepesh-ef for whom the tomb was constructed—standing behind his father, holding a ceremonial fan and wearing the sidelock of youth. The detail of the scene of RAMESES III CLASPING HANDS WITH THE GOD IMSETY (*p. 81*) again demonstrates a Ramesside interest in individualization. The eyes and lips of the monarch are distinctive and in sharp contrast to the more idealized features of the god. The detailed care with which these scenes are carved and painted can be seen in the treatment of the king's *nemes* headdress and fingernails. In the brilliant scene of RAMESES III CLASPING HANDS WITH PTAH-TENEN, FATHER OF THE GODS (*below*), the god's flesh is a vivid green, ritualistically representing this manifestation of the God Ptah as the verdure of new life emerging from the subsiding waters of the primeval flood.

RAMESES III CLASPING HANDS
WITH PTAH-TENEN, FATHER
OF THE GODS
Painted raised relief.
Antechamber, Tomb of Amen-hor-khepesh-ef,
Valley of the Queens (No. 85).
Dynasty XX (1190–1160 B.C.)
The accompanying text grants Rameses III many jubilees and eternal kingship similar to those previously granted Horus, son of Isis. Behind the king appears his son Amen-hor-khepesh-ef, holding a plumed fan. He is titled Overseer of Steeds.

V THEBES

TEMPLE OF LUXOR.

Egyptian temples were never intended to be completed during the reign of any given pharaoh. They were constantly being repaired, enlarged, and rebuilt by successive rulers. The Temple of Luxor dates from the New Kingdom and is primarily the result of the architectural activities of Kings Amenhotep III and Rameses II. It was dedicated to the Theban triad of Amun, his consort Mut, and their child Khonsu, and was called Ipet Resyt by the ancient Egyptians. The God Amun was obliged to travel from Karnak to Luxor in celebration of the Feast of the New Year, whose rites were celebrated in the Temple of Luxor. Remains of a ceremonial roadway, the WESTERN DROMOS (*pp. 85 and 87*), which led to the Temple of Khonsu at Karnak to the north are still preserved. This is lined on both sides by a series of sphinxes inscribed for King Nectanebo of Dynasty XXX; these sphinxes, with human heads, replaced the original ram-headed sphinxes of the New Kingdom. At the end of the Dromos stood two obelisks with the titles and name of Rameses II, one of which was given to France in 1831 by Mohammed Ali and re-erected on the Place de la Concorde in Paris in 1836. Beyond the obelisks were six colossal statues of Rameses II, the two flanking the entrance

WESTERN DROMOS
Temple of Luxor,
New Kingdom [Dynasties XVIII-XIX]
(1550–1190 B.C.)
The Pylon, obelisk and statues date from the reign of Rameses II (1290–1220 B.C.)

representing him sitting, and the other four showing him in striding attitude, of which only one remains. The pylon itself is decorated with scenes of his Hittite campaign and the Battle of Kadesh. The four rectangular recesses in the towers held the wooden flagstaffs from which the pennants flew, in honor of Amun, which means "the invisible one."

The pylon opens onto the Court of Rameses II, which contains a shrine for the barques of Amun, Mut and Khonsu. Along the rear wall, flanking the entrance to the partially destroyed pylon of Amenhotep III are two colossal seated statues of Rameses II, along the sides of whose legs are smaller images of his chief queen Nefertari represented as Hathor. Behind these statues lies the GREAT COLONNADE (*above*), whose roof was supported by the two rows each of seven columns, each 65½ feet tall, and crowned by capitals in the shape of open papyrus umbels. This Colonnade leads to the COURT OF AMENHOTEP III (*p. 90*), which is surrounded by two rows of shorter columns in the form of closed papyrus buds. The Hypostyle Hall begins immediately with the southern colonnade of the Court, and beyond is a series of smaller shrines including an Offering Chamber whose walls depict various rituals involving King Amenhotep III and the Gods Amun and Min. The Sanctuary proper in which the barques of gods came to rest during the principal festivals was built by Amenhotep III, but was repaired and restored by Alexander the Great. The Romans appropriated the Vestibule and trans-

P. 86
THE GREAT COLONNADE
Temple of Luxor,
New Kingdom [Dynasties XVIII-XIX]
(1550–1190 B.C.)

P. 87
SPHINXES OF THE WESTERN
DROMOS
Temple of Luxor.
Inscribed for King Nectanebo,
Dynasty XXX (380–342 B.C.)

COLONNADE, PROCESSIONAL WAY,
AND COURT OF AMENHOTEP III
Temple of Luxor.
Dynasties XVIII and XIX (1550–1190 B.C.)
At lower right, the Mosque of Abu el-Haggag.

89

formed it into a chapel devoted to the imperial cult. The fresco decoration, in Roman style, is still visible, if imperfectly preserved, and is among the finest examples of Roman painting in Upper Egypt.

At the northern end of the COLONNADE OF THE PROCESSIONAL WAY AND COURT OF AMENHOTEP III (*pp. 88–89*) stands the Mosque of Abu el-Haggag with its gleaming white-washed walls. And among the least conspicuous of modern buildings to appear in Luxor during the past decade is the Luxor Museum of Ancient Egyptian Art. Begun in 1964, the structure was completed in 1969 and formally opened in 1975. The aim was to create a place in the heart of Thebes where Theban art could be exhibited to best advantage. Among the works presently on view in the Museum are the colossal head of King Amenhotep III (p. 91), the cross-legged Seated Scribe statue of Amenhotep, Son of Hapu (p. 92), the striding statue of King Tuthmosis III (p. 100), the block statue of the official Yamu-nedjeh (p. 103), and the painted limestone reliefs from the Temple of Tuthmosis III at Deir el-Bahari (pp. 104 – 105).

Theban art has been observed to have a character distinctive from that created in the Delta. This art was shaped in part by the geographic isolation enjoyed by Thebes in the Nile Valley of Upper Egypt, which insulated it from foreign influence. Consequently a strong tradition was maintained in the Theban workshops over a long period of time. During Dynasty XVIII Thebes had the unparalleled honor of being the religious and secular capital of Egypt. Royal and sacerdotal patronage of the arts fostered a climate of

COURT OF AMENHOTEP III
Eastern side,
Temple of Luxor.
Dynasty XVIII (1400–1370 B.C.)

HEAD OF AMENHOTEP III
Red granite.
Dynasty XVIII (ca. 1400 B.C.)
Luxor Museum (No. J 133).

excellence supported by almost unlimited resources. As a result, many of the Theban sculptures produced at that time rank among the greatest master-pieces of Egyptian art.

HEAD OF AMENHOTEP III. *Dynasty XVIII.* *Above*

The colossal red-granite head of King Amenhotep III was discovered in 1957 in his Mortuary Temple at Qurna on the West Bank of Thebes. In many respects, this head is characteristic of Theban art at its best. The modeling of the facial features is minimal. At first glance, the volume of the face appears to consist of an oval offset by the White Crown's kingpin shape. This sculpture, like most Egyptian statues, was created by sculptors who, anonymously in large teams, abraded the surface with harder rubbing stones and added a polish with a component of emery and quartz. On close inspection and with raking light—by which all Egyptian sculpture is ideally illuminated in museums—the seemingly unmodulated oval form of the head reveals that it was conceived and created as a series of broad and gently convex plains which merge subtly into one another. Notice how the cheeks are full and in fact set off from the eye sockets which retreat into the mass of stone and thereby

91

contrast with the chin which projects forward into space. Such abstraction, with incidental details subordinated to the overall design, is responsible for a simple elegance. The design is enhanced by the eyebrows and the so-called "cosmetic lines" which ring the long narrow eyes, and are treated as undifferentiated plastic bands applied right onto the surface of the stone. The lips, as is the rule for Egyptian sculptures of quality, are set off from the skin of the face by a sharply executed vermilion line; the corners of the mouth have been accented by drilling into the stone, which has left a depression at each corner. The king is shown wearing the ritualistic false beard, held in place by a chin strap—itself treated in the same plastic manner as the eyebrows—and the White Crown fronted by a *uraeus*, the sacred cobra. The intent of the image is certain. The king's statue, to which this head belonged, is represented with the attributes of Osiris, Lord of the West, appropriate for a representation which stood originally in the Funerary Temple of Amenhotep III. This statue was made during the second half of that king's reign. The interplay of the convex planes and their resultant elegance were characteristics maintained and exploited by the artists of Amenhotep's son and successor, Akhenaten.

AMENHOTEP, SON OF HAPU. *Dynasty XVIII.* *Below*

This statue must rank as one of the finest depictions of a private person from Dynasty XVIII. He is represented as a scribe whose crossed legs stretch his kilt taut to provide a handy surface upon which to lay his papyrus, the unrolled portion of which he holds in his left hand. His right hand once held

Right
GREAT HYPOSTYLE HALL
Temple of Amun, Karnak.
Dynasty XIX (1550–1190 B.C.)

AMENHOTEP, SON OF HAPU
Reign of Amenhotep III,
1400–1370 B.C.
Dynasty XVIII.
Luxor Museum (No. J.4).

Left
TEMPLE OF PTAH
The five Pylons,
North side of the Temple of Amun,
Karnak.
Begun by King Tuthmosis III,
Dynasty XVIII (1490–1440 B.C.)

the reed brush which served as his pen. His head leans forward and his intent gaze is cast into space, focusing all of his energies on the thoughts he is about to commit to paper. Over his left shoulder is part of his scribe's kit, consisting of a rectangular container into which circular wells of red and black pigments, used as ink, were stored. Amenhotep was one of those remarkable men, like Imhotep (see p. 29) and Heka-ib (p. 150) who distinguished themselves in the service of their sovereign, state, and peers. In addition to his other administrative duties, he served as director of the Royal Works, and is probably the man responsible for the two colossal statues in quartzite made for Amenhotep III, one of which is today known as the Colossus of Memnon in Western Thebes. His lord even permitted him to serve as an intercessor between the God Amun at Karnak and pilgrims to his temple. As is often the case with parts of highly revered effigies of major religious figures in all cultures, the surface of the papyrus and kilt on this statue has become worn by attrition from the numerous reverential caresses accorded it by the pious through the centuries. The folds of fat of the chest and the heavy pectoral muscles are time-honored Egyptian conventions used as a sign of rank. Men so represented were habitually important administrators whose sedentary

FIRST COURT OF RECORDS
Reign of Tuthmosis III,
Temple of Amun, Karnak.
Dynasty XVIII (1490–1440 B.C.)

life is reflected in their physique. Their word and not the strength of their backs carried weight. A careful comparison between the face of Amenhotep, Son of Hapu, and of his sovereign Amenhotep III (p. 91) reveals how closely they parallel one another, particularly in the convexity of the planes and plasticity of the eyebrows and the cosmetic stripes of the eyes. However, the elongated face and pronounced chin are so characteristic of the many representations of Amenhotep Son of Hapu that this can be considered an actual portrait. The treatment of this statue exhibits the peculiar aesthetic of Egyptian art in which, unlike that of any other ancient land, extremely sculptural or plastic forms are combined with linear details.

TEMPLE OF AMUN, KARNAK. *Dynasties XVIII-XIX. p. 93*

In extent of space, number of individual temples, and variety of architectural detail no religious complex of any ancient culture can rival the sanctuaries of Karnak. In fact, this vast complex, parts of which are still being actively excavated and restored, is a tripartite ensemble of separate temple precincts,

GREAT HYPOSTYLE HALL
Reign of Amenhotep III (1400–1370).
Temple of Amun, Karnak.
Central aisle of the Hall, viewed from the doorway in foreground dating from the *Ptolemaic Dynasty (305–30 B.C.)*

Right
STATUE OF SAKHMET
Temple of Ptah,
Room to the right of the Sanctuary.
Karnak
Dynasty XVIII (1550–1305 B.C.)

each isolated from the other by its own mudbrick enclosure walls, and provided with its own sacred lake. North Karnak, the smallest of the three sectors, is devoted to Montu, god of war. To the south is the precinct of the Goddess Mut, consort of Amun-Re, King of the Gods and Lord of Thebes. At least five major structures have been identified here, in the least well-known quarter of the complex of Karnak, during the archeological campaigns conducted by The Brooklyn Museum since 1976.

Both the Precincts of Montu and of Mut have long been overshadowed by the Sanctuary of Amun, which stands between the two and comprises the largest area and the greatest number of structures at Karnak. Although the main temple is oriented east to west, there is a series of Southern Gateways on the axis of the Temple of Mut and the Avenue of Sphinxes connecting the Temples of Luxor with the Temple of Khonsu in the southeastern corner of the Precinct of Amun. The most awesome structure at Karnak is the GREAT HYPOSTYLE HALL (*pp. 93 and 96*). A courtyard, in which a single column remains from an edifice of Taharqa, containing sanctuaries erected by Sety II and Rameses III, is bounded on the east by the Second Pylon. The jambs of its doorway, which open into the Great Hypostyle, contain a now mutilated inscription describing the restorations of this area undertaken by the Ptolemies. The CENTRAL NAVE (*p. 93*) is formed by two rows of twelve columns, whose open papyrus umbel capitals supported impost blocks upon which the roofing slabs rested. The breadth of these capitals is so large that the impost blocks were hidden from sight when viewed from the ground. The result was a spectacular effect of a ceiling floating more than 75 feet above the floor of the Hypostyle Hall. It is estimated that fifty people could comfortably stand on one of those capitals. One hundred twenty-four columns with closed papyrus bud capitals complete the Hypostyle Hall, which measures 334 feet by 174 feet. Light and air were introduced into this space by a series of stone grills in a clerestory, some of which are still preserved (*p. 93*). The structure was originally undertaken by King Amenhotep III, but the Ramesside pharaohs subsequently covered virtually every inch of available space with their inscriptions and cartouches.

TEMPLE OF PTAH, KARNAK. *Dynasty XVIII.* *p. 94*

To the north of the great Temple of Amun, against the Enclosure Wall near the entrance to the Precinct of Montu, stands the Temple of the God Ptah, also oriented east to west. Although in an area remote from the main sanctuary, the Temple of Ptah exhibits several interesting features. The sanctuary proper was given its present shape during the reign of Tuthmosis III. It is approached by passing through five small pylons which are telescoped close onto one another (*p. 94*). The complex was restored during the Ptolemaic period, but the Ptolemies responsible for the work did not replace the original cartouches with their own. In one of the rare attempts to retain the original plan of the relief decoration and its inscriptions, the Ptolemies replaced the damaged or missing portions but inscribed them with the cartouches of the pharaohs under whom those sections were originally built. Such reverence for a predecessor's building is exceptional and outside the more widespread practice of claiming all repairs as one's own.

FIRST COURT OF RECORDS, KARNAK. *Dynasty XVIII.* *p. 95*

In this enormous complex of temples and subsidiary buildings, it should come as no surprise to discover among the surviving monuments at Karnak certain architectural details which attest to the creative genius of her planners. Just beyond the Sixth Pylon of the Temple of Amun lies the First Court of Records, erected by Tuthmosis III. Two granite pillars stand here, decorated with the Heraldic Plants of Upper and Lower Egypt. One, with the stylization of the grassy sedge, symbolic of Upper Egypt, appears on the right, or southern pillar; the other with that of the papyrus, symbolic of Lower Egypt, on the left, or northern pillar.

STATUE OF SAKHMET, TEMPLE OF PTAH, KARNAK.
Dynasty XVIII.   *p. 97*

In a chamber to the right of the sanctuary of the Temple of Ptah stands an over-life-size image of the Goddess Sakhmet. The leonine figure was considered in certain Egyptian cosmologies as a consort of Ptah. She was the patron deity of physicians as well. In this black granite statue, she wears a sun disc fronted by a uraeus on her head. Her face is framed by a tripartite wig whose ends fall over her shoulders onto her breasts. Wearing a broad collar, she is clothed in the tightly fitting, form-revealing sheath which gives the impression of nudity but whose hem is distinctly indicated just above the ankles. Such a garment, with slight variations, appears to have been the staple of a well-dressed Egyptian lady's wardrobe throughout the long history of Egyptian fashion. As a deity who grants life, she holds an *ankh* sign in her right hand; her left holds a papyrus scepter symbolizing her powers to promote the flourishing of beings.

THE RAMESEUM, WESTERN THEBES.
Dynasty XIX.   *Below*

While the Temples of Luxor and of Karnak were dedicated to the deities of the Egyptian pantheon, Western Thebes on the other side of the Nile was

THE RAMESEUM
Mortuary Temple of Rameses II.
Western Thebes.
Dynasty XIX (1290–1220 B.C.)

TEMPLE OF RAMESES III
Court and First Pylon,
Medinet Habu.
Dynasty XX (1190–1160 B.C.)

reserved, but not exclusively, for the funerary temples of the rulers and nobles, as well as for their tombs. The Rameseum was a large mortuary temple erected by Rameses II and dedicated to the God Amun. Today it is about half its original size, the vast magazines of mudbrick which once surrounded the structure having almost completely vanished and the monument itself used as a quarry. The scattered remains of the First Court are littered with the debris of the modern quarrymen. Of the Second Court, the four Osiride statues of Rameses II with their hands holding crooks and flails across their chests, are the most conspicuous. Here again, Rameses II took the opportunity of commemorating his exploits against the Hittites at the Battle of Kadesh on the walls of this section. In the upper registers, Rameses II celebrates the rituals of Min, God of Fertility and renewed life. The Hypostyle visible in the view shown here, is a smaller version of the one at Karnak. The remains of the largest free-standing sculpture known from ancient Egypt lie in the Forecourt. The length of one ear measures $3\frac{1}{2}$ feet; and from this and other fragments it is conjectured that the statue, representing Rameses II enthroned, as recorded by inscriptions, was almost 60 feet high and weighed nearly 1,000 tons. The prenomen of Rameses II was Weser-Maat-Re, which was preserved in Greek as Ozymandias. This is the statue that inspired Shelley's poem of that name.

TEMPLE OF RAMESES III, MEDINET HABU.
Dynasty XX. *Above*
To the south of the Rameseum and better preserved is the complex of buildings erected principally for Rameses III at Medinet Habu. The entrance to

99

this funerary temple is in the shape of a fortified gate, rather than a pylon, as one would expect. This architectural form may have been prompted by the unsettled times, with Egypt threatened by the invasions of the Sea Peoples. But the reliefs on the Gate represent Rameses III attempting to gain the favor of his harem, which is ironic because his very life was being threatened by a harem conspiracy. The association of women with this site remained strong. Just to the west of the Gate within the outer court lie the mortuary chapels dedicated to the divine consorts of Amun. These royal princesses, in theory wed to the God Amun, wielded great power during Dynasties XXV and XXVI. The corner of those chapels is visible at the bottom left of page 99. Beyond lies the First Pylon of the Temple of Rameses III. Each tower is decorated with a smiting scene similar to those at Edfu (p. 145), with Horus and Hathor here replaced by Amun and Waset, the latter the personification of Thebes.

STATUE OF TUTHMOSIS III
Reign of Tuthmosis III, 1490–1440 B.C.
Luxor Museum (No. J.2).

STATUE OF TUTHMOSIS III. *Dynasty XVIII.* *p. 100*

The combination of plastic forms and linear detail in Amenhotep Son of Hapu (p. 92) is again evident in one of the finest sculptures from Dynasty XVIII, King Tuthmosis III in striding attitude. The sheer plasticity of the modeling of the arms and torso conveys the sense of a vigorous male in the prime of life. The swelling flesh of the body is contrasted with the textured pleats of the kilt and those of the *nemes*-headdress. The false beard, with its rippled contours and linearly rendered strands of hair, acts as a transitional barrier so that the modeling of the face does not compete with that of the torso. The face itself is as idealized as the torso but the characteristic dip at the root of the nose preserves the physiognomic traits of the Tuthmosides, and the name of the king appearing in the cartouche serving as the buckle of the kilt belt makes the identification certain. The overall idealization of the face and torso are intentional. By disguising nature's flaws, the king strides forward in unblemished vigor as a god incarnate, unaffected by the ravages of time.

STRIDING FIGURE OF AN UNKNOWN MAN
Painted sandstone.
Dynasty XVIII (1567–1320 B.C.)
Luxor Museum (No. J.1).

STRIDING FIGURE OF AN UNKNOWN MAN. *Dynasty XVIII.* *Left*

Egyptian sculptors, trained in workshops, learned their craft as apprentices in schools which often had long traditions. Styles of earlier periods could be perpetuated with subtle yet detectable variations, a conscious imitation of an older style which has been labeled "archaizing." The pose, attitude and modeling of this painted sandstone statue are indebted to Old Kingdom models (see p. 27). The wig and facial features, however, suggest a date near the middle of Dynasty XVIII for this anonymous personage, who proudly strides forward exhibiting his gold ornaments. Bracelets and armlets are not uncommon as male accessories in ancient Egypt, but the gold collar worn by this figure is a military decoration of the highest order called "Gold of Honor," awarded during a specific, solemn ceremony. The excellent state of the color on this statue is remarkable and serves as a reminder that all Egyptian sculptures were originally intended to be richly colored.

BLOCK STATUE OF YAMU-NEDJEH. *Dynasty XVIII.* *p. 103*

Certain statues of private people made during the reign of Tuthmosis III are characterized by an idealization with somewhat different overtones, as exemplified by the statue of Yamu-nedjeh. He is represented squarely seated in squatting position on the ground, his garment completely enveloping his body, with only the head and hands emerging from the block. This is a uniquely Egyptian convention. Scholarly opinion is divided on the exact nature of the block statue. Some maintain that by retaining the cubic configuration of the stone from which it was carved, a low center of gravity would prevent it from being toppled. Others claim the shape was intended to represent the god arising from the primeval mound at the dawn of creation and that the deceased, so represented, would be assured of resurrection. The aesthetic of the block statue rests solely in the configuration of its contour, which in this superb example allows the shape of the legs, thighs, back, and shoulders to be revealed beneath the garment. The long inscription on the front of the garment informs us that Yamu-nedjeh accompanied his sovereign, Tuthmosis III, on military campaigns across the Euphrates River and erected two pairs of obelisks for his king at Karnak. So favored was this official that Tuthmosis III probably allowed this statue to be erected in his funerary temple at Qurna. The calm, tranquil expression on his idealized face and the slightly heavenward position of his head enable this effigy to be in eternal communication with his deified sovereign and the deities of the Egyptian pantheon.

SHRINE OF HATHOR, DEIR EL-BAHARI.
Dynasty XVIII.
Left

All the monuments described above were originally painted in bright colors. Some idea of their original appearance can be gleaned by looking at the Shrine of Hathor, built by Tuthmosis III in the northern corner of the Dynasty XI Temple at Deir el-Bahari. This shrine is dedicated to the cult of the Goddess Hathor, the divine nurse of kings, in her manifestation as the Cow-who-issues-forth-from-the-Mountain. A cave ten feet long and eight feet high was excavated in the mountain at the rear of the temple, and sandstone blocks were cut to size and placed to form the walls. Two huge blocks of stone, five feet each in length, were carved as arches and added to form the ceiling. The walls were then carved in low relief and painted. The shrine housed an image of King Tuthmosis III standing beneath the head of the Hathor Cow, represented as emerging from a thicket.

Although Hathor is the primary deity of the shrine, Amun, her consort, is

Left
SHRINE OF HATHOR
Reign of Tuthmosis III, 1490–1440 B.C.
Formerly in Deir el-Bahari.
Moved to Cairo Museum (No. JE 38575).

BLOCK STATUE OF YAMU-NEDJEH
Reign of Tuthmosis III, 1490–1440 B.C.
Luxor Museum (No. J.3).

THE FERTILITY GOD MIN
Fragment of painted relief from the
Temple of Amun, Deir el-Bahari, erected
by Tuthmosis III (1490–1440 B.C.), and
restored by Horemheb (1330–1305 B.C.)
Luxor Museum (No. J. 139).

equally prominent. He is represented, enthroned, on the back wall, being offered cool water and incense by the king (p. 102). In exchange for these offerings, according to the inscriptions, Amun offers the king "all life, prosperity, stability, and joy." The right wall contains several scenes. At the far end, Hathor, in a tightly-fitting sheath dress, is seen approaching King Tuthmosis III, standing in a traditional pose. The central panel is a translation in two dimensions of this shrine and its cult statue. Hathor, as the cow goddess with the sun disc, is shown emerging from a cloth-covered pavilion, with Tuthmosis standing below her head. A smaller figure kneeling and nursing at the cow's udder again represents Tuthmosis III. When the son of Amenhotep III, Akhenaten, established his religious program, the name and images of the God Amun were obliterated. This small shrine was subjected to the same iconoclasm, and the word Amun, even when used as a compound in the name of Tuthmosis' daughter Merit-Amun, was expunged from the wall. At some later date, after the return to orthodoxy, the name and image of Amun was restored to the once desecrated monuments.

THE GOD MIN and TUTHMOSIS III, TEMPLE OF AMUN, DEIR EL-BAHARI. *Dynasty XVIII.* *Above & Right*

Brightly painted figures against white backgrounds seem to characterize a prevailing taste of Tuthmosis III at Western Thebes. Thousands of pieces

TUTHMOSIS III WEARING THE ATEF CROWN
Fragment of painted relief from the Temple of Amun, Deir el-Bahari, erected by Tuthmosis III (1490–1440 B.C.)
Luxor Museum (No. J.140).

with this color scheme have been unearthed at Deir el-Bahari in recent years by the Polish Expedition to that site. It is speculated that they belong to the now destroyed Temple of Amun built by Tuthmosis on a rocky ledge southwest of the famous Funerary Temple of Queen Hatshepsut at Deir el-Bahari. Some of the pieces are in their original state, and others have been subjected to ancient restorations. In the first category is the profile representation of KING TUTHMOSIS III WEARING THE ATEF CROWN of Osiris and the symbolic beard of divinity (*above*). Dating from the time of the king, the raised relief has been cut and colored with a sure hand, and great care lavished on the execution of the details. The profile with its aquiline nose set off from the forehead provides an individualistic feature in an otherwise idealized depiction, reminiscent of that found in the face of the striding statue of the king in the Luxor Museum (p. 100). On the other hand, the representation of the FERTILITY GOD MIN (*p. 104*), which was recut and repainted during the period of the ancient restoration of the Temple, lacks the vitality of the portrait of the king, and is the product of the post-Amarnan period. It is only by such careful scrutiny of all parts of the same temple that definitive stylistic criteria are evolved for determining the aesthetic characteristics of given periods in Egyptian art. The fragmentary nature of these reliefs is attributed to a rock slide which occurred subsequent to the restoration, some time near the end of the New Kingdom.

VI THE THEBAN NECROPOLIS

In contrast to the royal tombs in the Valley of the Kings (pp. 50–72), whose rituals were celebrated in temples in the Theban plain, are the so-called tombs of the nobles. Those constructed during Dynasty XVIII are adorned with scenes of daily life that are so precise in their portrayal of social intercourse, that the ancient Egyptians emerge as human beings with the same passions, emotions, and feelings which mankind throughout history has experienced. These scenes capture the Egyptians at work and at play and imbue them with such vitality that one cannot but conclude that the ancient Egyptians were, in fact, human beings in whom we can often recognize ourselves. These tombs are confined to three cemeteries which are separated from one another by a considerable distance. The northernmost of these three are the tombs of El-Kokha, situated to the south of a hill of the same name. Members of the Theban aristocracy of both Dynasty XVIII and XIX were

TWO SOUTHERNERS RESTRAINING A GIRAFFE
Tomb of Rekh-mi-re,
Theban necropolis (No. 100).
Reigns of Tuthmosis III and Amenhotep II, 1490–1410 B.C.

106

SCULPTORS AT WORK
ON A COLOSSAL STATUE
Tomb of Rekh-mi-re,
Theban necropolis (No. 100).
Reigns of Tuthmosis III and Amenhotep II.
1490–1410 B.C.

interred here. To the southwest lie the tombs of Sheikh Abd el-Qurna which are situated in a hill to the north of the Rameseum. The third group, built mostly by the artisans and necropolis officials of Dynasty XIX and XX, are at Deir el-Medineh, due east of the Valley of the Queens. In plan, these tombs are all variations of a type which consists of a forecourt, a pillared hall, and a corridor in which statues of the deceased and his favorite relatives were carved. Additional chambers could be added. The cult of the deceased was celebrated in an open court before the tomb to which offerings were brought.

TOMB OF REKH-MI-RE. *Dynasty XVIII.* pp. 106–109

Not far from the Rameseum is the tomb of Rekh-mi-re, a court official who served as vizier in the reigns of both Tuthmosis III and Amenhotep II. During that time many foreign embassies, all bearing as tribute the characteristic products of their native lands, sought audiences at the Egyptian court. As vizier, it was Rekh-mi-re's duty to receive these delegations, some of which came from as far away as the islands of the Aegean and the Land of Punt (present-day Somali). Among the more important were the Nubians, who dispatched embassies bearing gold, skins, and live animals of the more exotic species found in the heart of Africa. The depiction of the Nubians in this tomb is more lively than that of other foreign peoples, as shown in this detail of TWO SOUTHERNERS RESTRAINING A GIRAFFE (*p. 106*) by pulling on ropes attached to its feet. Despite the contingencies of the space and the Egyptian conventions of scale, the giraffe does appear to tower over his captors. The giraffe is depicted, not as a fabulous beast, but rather as a zoological specimen whose proportions and coloring are based upon a careful observation of

107

nature. Such depictions clearly demonstrate that the ancient Egyptian artists could accurately represent what their eyes beheld. A touch of humor is added to the scene by the inclusion of the simian who uses the long neck of the giraffe as a tree trunk on which he climbs. Care was also lavished on the costumes of the Nubians themselves. The figure to the right wears an elaborate necklace while his companion is dressed in a patterned loin cloth. Each has a different coiffure as well.

Among Rekh-mi-re's many duties was the inspection of workmen and architects busy on royal commissions. The technique employed by the Egyptians in making their statues is revealed in the scene of Sculptors at work on a Colossal Statue (*p. 107*), depicted on the south wall of the Tomb of Rekh-mi-re. Without iron tools and the benefit of advanced technology, the Egyptians were able to create masterpieces of sculpture such as that of King Tuthmosis III (p. 100). The basic operation consisted of abrading the block of the statue with a stone of a geologically harder rating, assisted by quartz and emery compounds. Here a team of artists is engaged in making a colossal figure of a seated king. A scaffold has been erected to enable them to work on the top. The kneeling figure at the right holds a whitish grazing tool, which he moves back and forth over the surface of the headdress to shape it. His companion is adding linear detail to the royal *uraeus* on the brow of the statue. The unfinished state of the statue is indicated by the flecks of red with which the salmon-colored figure is covered. The scene of which this is a detail includes also the completion of a pylon, with the result that

METALWORKERS
Tomb of Rekh-mi-re,
Theban necropolis (No. 100).
*Reigns of Tuthmosis III and Amenhotep II,
1490–1410 B.C.*

this architectural program resembled that of the main pylon at the Temple of Luxor with its seated colossi (p. 85).

Rekh-mi-re was also responsible for overseeing the workshops of the metalworkers and carpenters. In a detail showing METALWORKERS (*p. 108*), an attempt has been made to convey the idea of enormous activity. The artist divided the main register into smaller groups by introducing two subsidiary groundlines, so that four individual operations are shown. At lower left, two workmen, each standing on foot-bellows, attempt to build up the temperature of an open furnace. When the proper temperature has been reached, the bellows are pulled away by the ropes attached to them. The scene at lower right shows the bellows moved to one side with their long nozzles lying near the edge of the fire. Having removed the bellows, the workmen then heat the metal in a crucible cradled between rocking rods. The spout on the pouring crucible faces to the right. In the scene above, two more workmen are busy with another fire, while a third figure stirs the flame and appears to be adding charcoal from the pile before him. To the left, a second pair lifts a crucible on to the fire. The molten metal is now ready to be poured.

In scenes showing METALWORKERS SHAPING VESSELS (*p. 109*), the convention of secondary groundlines is again employed. The two lower registers of this large scene show craftsmen working on various stages of the production itself. In the middle register, the tools used in this operation are rendered along with the fire for annealing the metal in the field between the workmen to the right. The top register shows carpenters at work. The figure

METALWORKERS SHAPING VESSELS
Tomb of Rekh-mi-re,
Theban necropolis (No. 100).
*Reigns of Tuthmosis III and Amenhotep II,
1490–1410 B.C.*

109

to the right is occupied with sawing his stock into thin planks, two of which are shown just behind him. To the left, a team of woodworkers operates a bow drill in finishing touches on a lion-shaped funerary bier. Under the bier is a chest which they have already completed. The Egyptians were the finest woodworkers in all antiquity. Their furniture exhibits the complete repertoire of joints and doweling, with a quality of craftsmanship matching that of finest eighteenth-century European cabinetwork.

The figural style in the Tomb of Rekh-mi-re marks a departure from certain Egyptian conventions. The scenes of the metalworkers and of the carpenters rely on a predominance of profile views in which the frontality of the chest, a fundamental element in Egyptian simultaneity, is slightly modified. The breadth of the torso is narrowed, occasionally only one arm is visible, and more often both arms appear to emerge from the same socket. Ungainly as these figures may thus appear, they do represent one step in the evolution of a more naturalistic approach to the human figure.

BIRDS IN A MARSH, TOMB OF AMEN-EM-HET.
Dynasty XVIII.   *Right*

Naturalism was to characterize the development of the arts during Dynasty XVIII, and may be directly related to the medium employed. In traditional relief carving, an outline scribe was first required to draw the scene on the wall to be decorated. The sculptors then translated the drawing into relief. With painting, on the other hand, the initial work of the outline scribe was eventually deemed unnecessary and the painters were able to work directly on the stucco coating from their pattern books and sketches. The brush was more immediate than the chisel, more controllable, and more conducive to spontaneous choices of design. Consequently, it is in the painted Theban tombs of Dynasty XVIII that the stages of naturalism can be best observed. One of the more remarkable of these early attempts at naturalism and the concomitant virtuosity of its brush work is the fragment of a swamp scene from the Tomb of Amen-em-het who served as a scribe, a counter of the grain of Amun, and a steward for the vizier under Tuthmosis III. Only a small section of the birds in this scene is preserved but, when compared to the similar scene from Assuan (p. 155), its value is immediately evident. The birds are carefully modeled after nature, although their wings have been rotated against the planes of their bodies. Nevertheless, a sense of sudden flight prompted by the unexpected approach of the fowler is nicely conveyed. The shading on the bodies of both the crane and hoopoe with dappled, superimposed, and juxtaposed colors belongs to a painterly tradition which is rarely recognized.

TOMB OF SEN-NUFER. *Dynasty XVIII.*   *pp. 112–116*

The scenes discussed so far are isolated and removed from their contexts. Some idea of the scope of the decoration and placement of the scenes in the tomb of a nobleman is obtained by examining the Tomb of Sen-nufer. Under King Amenhotep II, Sen-nufer served both as mayor of Thebes and as overseer of the Gardens of Amun. In the PILLARED HALL (*p. 112–113*), Sen-nufer is represented on each of the faces of the piers, seated and attended by

Pp. 112–113
TOMB OF SEN-NUFER,
PILLARED HALL
Theban necropolis (No. 96).
Reign of Amenhotep II, 1440–1410 B.C.

BIRDS IN A MARSH
Tomb of Amen-em-het,
Theban necropolis (No. 82).
Reign of Tuthmosis III, 1490–1440 B.C.

110

members of his family. His wife, Merit, adjusts the amulet on his chest and offers a broad collar. On the far wall, two jackals representing Anubis recline on shrines above the niches for the sarcophagus. The tomb is designed in part as a festival pavilion with a ceiling of brightly painted cloth. The remainder has been carved and decorated to resemble a lush grape arbor. Already at this early date the Egyptians had seized upon the funerary significance of that plant, anticipating the funerary cult of the Greek Dionysus by several centuries. As mayor of Thebes, Sen-nufer subtly adopted certain royal motifs for use in his own tomb. In a PURIFICATION SCENE (*below*) Sen-nufer and his wife are being sprinkled with holy water by a *sem*-priest, identified by his leopard-skin costume. Sen-nufer, with earrings, goatee, gold of honor ornaments and other jewelry, faces the priest. His garments are of the finest linen and are so sheer that his kilt and legs are visible from beneath his overgarment. He holds a formal bouquet in his hand which was called "*ankh*" in Egyptian. By means of this appellation, an elaborate pun is achieved. Sen-nufer thereby holds the *ankh* (sign of life), which is reserved for deities. The conceit is completed by his wife who holds a *menat*, or ritual rattle, across her

PURIFICATION SCENE
Tomb of Sen-nufer,
Theban necropolis (No. 96).
Reign of Amenhotep II, 1440–1410 B.C.

114

SEN-NUFER SEATED ON A DAIS
Tomb of Sen-nufer,
Theban necropolis (No. 96).
Reign of Amenhotep II, 1440–1410 B.C.

breast and a sistrum and lettuce leaf at her side. She is thereby equipped with the attributes of certain goddesses, notably Hathor. The resulting composition can be compared to that of a divine couple before whom a priest or king officiates. The scene is rendered inoffensive to royal sensibilities because of its understatement and use of visual puns, in which the Egyptians took extreme delight. The inscriptions praise the couple for their work in the various sanctuaries of the God Amun.

A similarly constructed scene shows SEN-NUFER SEATED ON A DAIS (*above*). Behind Sen-nufer is a sycamore tree, sacred to Hathor, and he is sniffing a lotus blossom. By a similar conceit, already established by the Middle Kingdom, the lotus becomes a pun for the *ankh* sign so that Sen-nufer effectively grants life to himself. His wife, according to tradition, is represented in smaller scale but on her own dais. Her far arm reaches behind and around the legs of her husband which she embraces. Before the couple is an offering table upon which are three vases, their tops sealed with clay sealings represented by the black tops.

Some of the scenes from the Pillared Hall in the Tomb of Sen-nufer are

remarkably well planned and skillfully executed. The artists were given free rein to pursue their creative talents. Those scenes contrast sharply with the style and execution of the strictly religious scenes of this tomb. The representation of the MYTHICAL VOYAGE TO ABYDOS (*above*) appears to be the work of a less skilled artist. By comparison, the figures appear stiff and less accomplished. Sen-nufer and Merit sit beneath a canopied cabin on the deck of their vessel. Before them is a table heaped high with breads and vegetables, funerary offerings for the deceased. A priest, offering cool water, presides at this ceremony, while a smaller helmsman guides the craft on its way. The Nile is represented as a blue-green band on which white zigzags, actually the hieroglyph *n*, symbolize its rippling waters. The inscriptions with the cabin translate, "The deceased, the mayor of Thebes, Sen-nufer, the justified. The housewife, Merit." Above the helmsman is a legend for funerary offerings which include, "1000 loaves of bread, 1000 bottles of beer, one thousand of every thing good and pure, all offerings."

MYTHICAL VOYAGE TO ABYDOS
Tomb of Sen-nufer,
Theban necropolis (No. 96).
Reign of Amenhotep II, 1440–1410 B.C.

TOMB OF KHA-EM-HET. *Dynasty XVIII.* *pp. 117, 118*

Since the Egyptians practiced sympathetic magic by which the representation of an object was believed to become the object itself, these tombs are provided with statues of the deceased and whatever members of his family he wished to be represented. What such statues look like in place is shown on page 139. In this tomb, the STATUES OF KHA-EM-HET AND HIS WIFE (*p. 117*) are found at the rear of the Inner Hall. Kha-em-het was the superintendent of the Royal Granaries under King Amenhotep III, when Egypt was at the height of her power and wealth. The courtiers were able to select the ablest of artists to work on their tombs. These statues were carved from the living rock. The Lady of the House, in the detail below from the Kha-em-het Tomb, is wearing a wide wig, which frames her face and focuses on her features. The cosmetic brow and paint stripes around the eyes are formal elements which combine with the sculptural treatment of the nose, lips, and chin in creating a likeness of the woman depicted. Characteristic for works of exceptional quality is the presence of the vermilion line which separates the flesh of the lips from the skin of the face. To the right one can see the so-called "Offering List," rectangular compartments, each of which contains in hieroglyphs the name of a food, article of clothing, or luxury item, which could be used by the deceased in the Hereafter. The figure of Kha-em-het himself is somewhat better preserved although it has suffered damage from a fire. Over his broad collar is a necklace consisting of the double heart. The delicacy of the carving of the individual locks on the double echelon wig is noteworthy. The face is modeled in broad, smooth planes with the eyes set obliquely in the face. The shape of the eyes and their plastic, cosmetic lines and paint stripes compare favorably to similar features on other statues made during the reign of Amenhotep III. The finely modeled lips are themselves set off by a vermilion line, which is a feature found exclusively in works of outstanding craftsmanship. The Tomb of Kha-em-het is decorated with bold, raised reliefs whose contours are almost perpendicular to the plane of the wall. The figures readily detach from the neutral background and project strongly forward, as in the scene of KHA-EM-HET DRESSING (*p. 118*). To the right stands a group of solicitous retainers in attitudes of respect. The use of overlap is effective in

STATUES OF KHA-EM-HET, right
AND HIS WIFE, left
Tomb of Kha-em-het,
Theban necropolis (No. 57).
Reign of Amenhotep III, 1400–1370 B.C.

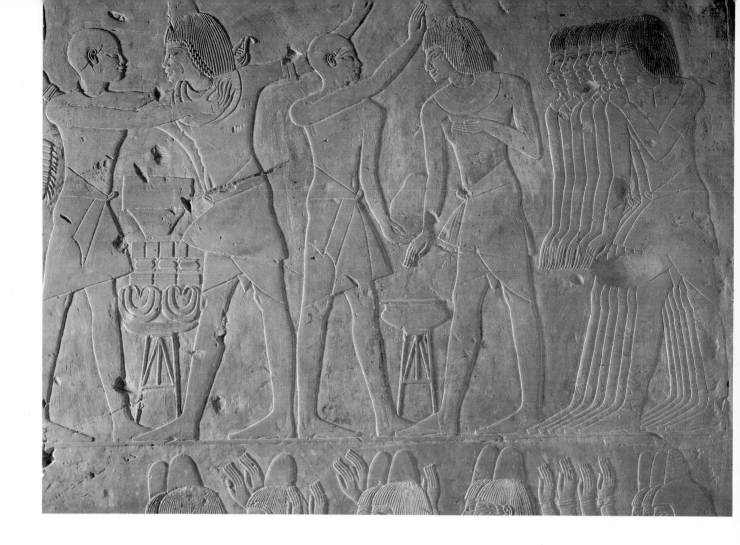

KHA-EM-HET DRESSING
Tomb of Kha-em-het,
Theban necropolis (No. 57).
Reign of Amenhotep III, 1400–1370 B.C.

achieving a sense of depth; the artist, by that convention, is representing a row of six men standing shoulder to shoulder. In front of them Kha-em-het leans forward so that his valet can fix an ointment cone onto his wig. Kha-em-het then proceeds to a dressing table, after first putting on his armlets. At left, one of the broad ceremonial necklaces has been selected from the group on a stand between Kha-em-het and a servant, and the latter is shown placing it around his master's neck. The two images of Kha-em-het himself in this vignette depict him as a vigorous adult at the right, and as a somewhat portly, older man at the left. The Egyptians were often concerned with depictions of the ages of man and habitually juxtaposed representations of the same individual at two different stages of his life. Kha-em-het, accordingly, performed his duties and rose to the rank of a high bureaucrat. One need only compare the treatment of this torso to that of the statue of Amenhotep, son of Hapu, to realize that the artists were working within a tradition (p. 92). Excessive weight was used as a sign of rank in Egyptian representations such as these.

FISHING AND FOWLING SCENE, TOMB OF MENNA.
Dynasty XVIII. p. 119–121

One of the most interesting representations of fishing and fowling is to be found in the Tomb of Menna. The type itself has a long history, but is here presented with a unique combination of formal conventions and naturalistic touches. Mirror images of Menna striding upon papyrus boats flank the central vertical mass representing the papyrus marsh. To the left, Menna holds up live fowl by the feet as decoys while his free hand, not visible, hurls throwsticks at the marsh birds. A servant, understandably in smaller scale, holds three birds by the wings. To the right, Menna, accompanied by a similar retainer, is shown harpooning fish. In order to paint the scene in the clearest, most unambiguous terms, the artists have transferred the action which occurs in the water beneath the boat to a hill of water which climbs the picture plane. The conventions of simultaneous views here have been pushed to the extreme. There is no doubt that Menna is about to harpoon the big one. The Nile appears as a blue band decorated with darker zigzags. Water plants and animals have then been represented as if they were cut-outs pasted against that band. The fishing activity has its counterpart in the water where a crocodile is landing its own catch just to the left of center. Menna's costume consists of a layered ensemble of fine, gossamer linen garments which, like that of Sen-nufer (p. 114), permit the undergarments and limbs to be visible. There is a distinct departure from formal conventions at the top of the papyrus marsh in the center of the scene (detail pp. 120–121). The papyrus umbels were painted directly on the stucco without the assistance of prelim-

FISHING AND FOWLING SCENE
Tomb of Menna,
Theban necropolis (No. 69).
Reign of Tuthmosis IV, 1415–1405 B.C.

FISHING AND FOWLING SCENE, detail
Tomb of Menna,
Theban necropolis (No. 69).
Reign of Tuthmosis IV, 1415–1405 B.C.

121

inary drawing by an outline scribe. The application of the paint in succession from the green at the stems to the ochre of the umbels is evident. As playful as the crocodile at the bottom is the *nems*, a small mammal like a mongoose, negotiating a stalk which begins to succumb to gravity as the diminutive creature nears the top. Equally arresting is the surefooted cat above who, having stalked its quarry, raises a paw to smite an unsuspecting duck. Such details are the result of repeated observations and allow us to appreciate the skills of the artists involved in their creation. The space at the top is occupied by waterfowl at whose necks the throwsticks are aimed. Five such weapons, looking like short, convex serpents, complete with head, are scattered across the field. Two have hit their respective marks and the birds upside down begin to fall earthward. Two butterflies flit about unconcerned with the plight of their feathered friends. The most interesting aspects in the Tomb of Menna are these incidental vignettes which are incorporated into the more formal scenes, but which are infinitely more amusing and telling.

HARVEST SCENES, TOMB OF MENNA.

Dynasty XVIII.   *pp. 122–126*

As a scribe of the fields and estate inspector perhaps under King Tuthmosis IV, Menna had first-hand experience with all aspects of agriculture and the human drama which unfolded during the course of his daily activities. In a scene of MEASURING THE CROP (*below*), Menna shares these experiences with the spectator on the walls of his tomb. To the left, an official, so indicated by the *was*-scepter he holds, accompanies a surveyor who, with a cord, measures the productive acreage of the wheat field. Taxes were levied according to yield and the collectors were extremely exact in their reckonings. The ubiquitous scribe accompanies this team; only his palette is visible at the

MEASURING THE CROP
Tomb of Menna,
Theban necropolis (No. 69).
Reign of Tuthmosis IV, 1415–1405 B.C.

extreme left edge of the illustration. In a scene of MEN CARRYING A BASKET OF WHEAT (*below*), the two farm hands seem to be engaged in idle chatter. To the right, a weary co-worker attempts to take a break by catnapping beneath the shade of a tree in order to escape the hot sun for a moment. The most interesting detail in this scene, however, is placed in the foreground, beneath the basket. In center stage, two gleaners have become involved in an altercation and have resorted to a hair-pulling contest. The vignette apparently reflects a common phenomenon because it is repeated a few reigns later in the reliefs sculpted for King Akhenaten. About 650 B.C. the powerful Fourth Prophet of Amun, Montu-em-hat, planned his own tomb at Western Thebes. It seems that he and his architects visited many of the older monuments, including the temples at Deir el-Bahari and this Tomb of Menna. Like King Akhenaten, he was moved by the depiction of the quarreling gleaners and had the vignette repeated in relief in his tomb, which is, incidentally, the largest private tomb at Thebes. Such repeating of certain motifs in more recent scenes is known as archaizing (see p. 97); this phenomenon demonstrates that the ancient Egyptians knew about their past and were ever ready to dip into that past when the opportunity for doing so presented itself. In the continuing scenes, RAKING THE WHEAT (*p. 124, bottom*) shows the grain, after being cut, being gathered up by two farm hands under the watchful eye of an official who is represented as an older man with a receding hairline. The latter seems impervious to the farmers' banter which, by the positions of their heads, is aimed directly at him. The two enormous piles, recalling the hieroglyph for "hill country," form another, somewhat obscure visual pun. There is also a THRESHING SCENE (*p. 124, top*) wherein the hooves of the cattle break up the grain. As a precaution at this stage of the work, the threshers have covered their heads. The GRAIN WINNOWERS (*p. 125, top*) now

MEN CARRYING A BASKET OF WHEAT
Tomb of Menna,
Theban necropolis (No. 69).
Reign of Tuthmosis IV, 1415–1405 B.C.

THRESHING SCENE
Tomb of Menna,
Theban necropolis (No. 69).
Reign of Tuthmosis IV, 1415–1405 B.C.

RAKING THE WHEAT
Tomb of Menna,
Theban necropolis (No. 69).
Reign of Tuthmosis IV, 1415–1405 B.C.

GRAIN WINNOWERS
Tomb of Menna,
Theban necropolis (No. 69).
Reign of Tuthmosis IV, 1415–1405 B.C.

COUNTING THE GRAIN
Tomb of Menna,
Theban necropolis (No. 69).
Reign of Tuthmosis IV, 1415–1405 B.C.

DELINQUENT TAXPAYER and
PUNISHED TAXPAYER
Tomb of Menna,
Theban necropolis (No. 69).
Reign of Tuthmosis IV, 1415–1405 B.C.

take over and with their fans toss the wheat into the air to separate the grain from the chaff. Here also their heads are covered. In the next scene of COUNT-ING THE GRAIN (*p. 125, below*), the grain, still piled high in the form of the "hill country" sign, is now ready for measuring the crop. Between the piles, four workers depicted as if to represent a row, scoop up bushels of grain. The scribe sitting on the pile to the right gives the count out loud as he gestures with his hand to emphasize the number of bushels measured. No less than five additional scribes record the count in an intricate system of checking so that there can be no doubt about the exact total of the yield. These records formed the basis for taxation, which was seldom evaded. The two following scenes demonstrate the forcefulness of the tax collectors. In the top register, a DELINQUENT TAXPAYER (*above*) is shown being manhandled by the tax col-lector, to whom the others show respect. Below, in a scene of a PUNISHED TAXPAYER, some sort of disagreement about the assessment has caused the taxpayer to be cast to the ground and bludgeoned by the collector, while the pleas of a sympathetic ally are for naught. Such scenes are revealing because they represent an almost universal feeling toward the tax collector which our times certainly seem to share. The figural style in this tomb is related to that of the Tomb of Rekh-mi-re (pp. 106–109), particularly with regard to the narrowing of the width between the shoulders in an attempt to render a more naturalistic profile, and capture the feeling for hands engaged in manual operations.

126

Right
GIRL MUSICIANS
Tomb of Nakht,
Theban necropolis (No. 52).
*Reign of Tuthmosis IV (?),
1415–1405 B.C.*

GIRL MUSICIANS. TOMB OF NAKHT.

Dynasty XVIII.   *p. 127*

Among the most skillfully executed of the painted tombs of Dynasty XVIII is the Tomb of Nakht. Nakht himself served as a scribe and functioned as a *wenuti*, a title the meaning of which is not clear. Although traditionally translated "astronomer," a *wenuti* might also have been a lay priest. In either case, the title rarely appears among officials of Dynasty XVIII and probably indicates that Nakht himself served in the lower strata of the Theban bureaucracy. It is also not certain under whose reign he flourished. If one accepts the theory that pattern books were used in the decoration of these tombs, the scenes of his tomb find their closest parallels in the sepulchers of officials who are known to have lived under either Amenhotep II or Tuthmosis IV. The effacing of the word "Amun," presumed to be the work of the Atenists, squares with the evidence just presented. One can assume that Nakht was active during the reign of Tuthmosis IV. Despite the elusive nature of facts of his biography, Nakht was able to engage artists of outstanding ability. The south side of the west wall of his tomb depicts a banquet scene at which a group of seated women enjoy the strains of a portly harpist who is represented with closed eyes, a convention for representing the state of inspiration. Below, a group of men sitting on chairs watch the performance of three girl musicians, which is one of the most accomplished vignettes to survive. The graceful trio play a double flute, a lute, and a harp. Note particularly the attention paid by the painter to their hands and the expressive positions of the fingers which recall the same kind of treatment in the Mem-

SED FESTIVAL DANCERS
Tomb of Kheru-ef,
Theban Necropolis (No. 192).
Reigns of Amenhotep III and Akhenaten, 1400–1360 B.C.

RITUAL DANCE
Tomb of Kheru-ef,
Theban necropolis (No. 192).
*Reigns of Amenhotep III and Akhenaten,
1400–1360 B.C.*

phite tomb of Horemheb (p. 34). The fingers bend to the rhythm of their music. The flautist and harpist wear the gossamer ensemble of fine linen which reveals the forms of their bodies beneath. These dressed figures form a frame and a foil for the nude lute player between them. She wears only a broad collar, bracelets and a girdle slung from her hips. The spectator is thereby treated to a sensual scene, which was the intent of the artist. Compositionally, the trio reflect a considerable amount of planning. The direction of movement proceeds from left to right; yet, the flow is interrupted by the central figure who turns her head back, against the grain, to communicate with the flautist. The three are thereby linked together by a tight composition whose design is pleasant.

TOMB OF KHERU-EF. *Dynasty XVIII.* *pp. 128, 129*

Of the over four hundred private tombs in Western Thebes, only a handful, dating from the New Kingdom, are decorated with relief sculpture. Of those, the Tomb of Kheru-ef is the most important. Kheru-ef lived during the reigns of Amenhotep III and of his son Akhenaten and served as the Chief Steward of Queen Tiye, the wife of the former and mother of the latter. His exalted position enabled him to participate in many important ceremonies, particularly since Tiye, as the chief and later dowager queen of Egypt, exercised considerable influence and authority at the courts of both her husband and son. Many of these ceremonies are represented on the walls of this tomb. They are of a religious or of an historical nature and include vignettes not known from other monuments. As a result, these scenes provide valuable

p. 130–131
SEN-NEDJEM AND HIS WIFE IN
THE FIELDS OF IARU
Tomb of Sen-nedjem,
Theban necropolis (No. 1).
Dynasty XIX (1305–1200 B.C.)

129

material for an understanding of the early reign of the heretic King Akhenaten. Kheru-ef apparently did not subscribe to his new sovereign's religious reforms. His tomb is unfinished and parts of it were deliberately destroyed by the Atenists. The raised relief decoration of the Second Court commemorates one of the *sed* or jubilee festivals celebrated by Amenhotep III. These festivals were theoretically held every thirty years but were more frequent in practice. The third *sed*-festival held in the thirty-sixth regnal year of King Amenhotep III is recorded in the relief. These festivals consisted of a series of rituals which magically rejuvenated the king and assured the continued vigor of his reign. On the north wall, Kheru-ef presents gifts to his sovereigns, the king and queen, and acts as the chief official in the ceremony of erecting the Djed Pillar. The Djed Pillar is a schematized representation of the human spinal column, and symbolized stability since Egyptian physicians from early times had determined that the erect posture of man was due in part to this skeletal part of the body. By transference, erecting the symbol of anatomical stability became a metaphor for assuring the continued harmony and order of the pharaoh's reign. Kheru-ef himself holds one of the ropes used in raising the Djed Pillar. The ceremony was accompanied, as were many Egyptian rituals by song and dance, represented in this detail of SED FESTIVAL DANCERS (*p. 128*) from the relief celebrating the raising of the pillar. The carving is in very bold relief with a considerable amount of interior modeling. The calf and thighs of the second dancer from the right, for example, are revealed through her skirt. Several of the dancers wear criss-crossed straps over their chests. Due to the conventions of simultaneity the chest is shown in front view, as are the straps. The breasts, however, have been rotated so that only one is shown, and that in profile. Compare this treatment of the female torso to that of the lute player in the Tomb of Nakht (p. 127), which is one of the rare examples of an Egyptian female figure in a two-dimensional representation in which both breasts are naturalistically rendered in front view. The inscription in the field in front of the left pair of hand-clappers reads, "or the erection of the Djed Pillar," and confirms the identification of the scene. In another scene of the same relief similarly clad dancers wearing long wigs are engaged in a more frenetic RITUAL DANCE (*p. 129*), displaying a choreography in which the flowing movement of the dancers' arms, with hands bent out at the wrists, is combined with the swaying of their long tresses. The rows of hieroglyphs below their feet contain the cartouches naming Amenhotep III.

TOMB OF SEN-NEDJEM. *Dynasty XIX.* *pp. 130–132*

With the advent of the Ramesside pharaohs of Dynasty XIX, the decoration of the tombs of the nobles at Thebes departs in technique and subject matter from those of Dynasty XVIII. The majority of the scenes are occupied with religious subjects, almost forcing the disappearance of scenes of daily life. All are painted on stucco with a predominantly yellow-orange background on which the numerous spells associated with the rituals depicted are painted in black. The Tomb of Sen-nedjem serves as an introduction to the private tombs of Dynasty XIX. On the far wall, beneath a vaulted ceiling, SEN-NEDJEM STANDING IN ADORATION BEFORE A SHRINE (*p. 132*), he is shown wearing a pleated kilt, and an ointment cone on his head, and accompanied by his wife. The roof of the shrine is lined with a frieze of cobras on whose heads are sun discs. Thirteen gods of the Underworld, brightly painted against a white background, occupy the shrine's interior in two rows. Osiris, at the top left, holds the pre-eminent position among those thirteen deities. The tympanum above shows a pair of confronted jackals of Anubis, both sitting upon mastabas. On the wall to the right, Anubis, as an anthropomor-

phic deity, attends the sarcophagus of Sen-nedjem lying on a lion-shaped bier within a pavilion. The accompanying texts come from a Ramesside recension of *The Book of the Dead*. The formalism of the scene and the stiff poses of the figures do not compare with the more naturalistic attempts of the figural style of the tombs of Dynasty XVIII. Nevertheless, such reserve is appropriate for the subject matter depicted since the very nature of religious representations demands a degree of restraint and reserve on the part of the artist. The tympanum of the facing wall in the Tomb of Sen-nedjem (p. 130) depicts baboons worshiping the barque of the falcon-headed sun god, which sets the scene at dawn, the moment of the sun god's rebirth in the new day. In the scenes below are depicted SEN-NEDJEM AND HIS WIFE IN THE FIELDS OF IARU after their resurrection (*p. 130*). There they toil on the farm, which itself is a symbol of resurrection. Just as the crops are sown and harvested and re-emerge after a second sowing, so too the deceased, after death, was believed to be reborn in the Hereafter. The Egyptians maintained that life after death was similar to life on earth and that many of the occupations of this world had to be performed in the Hereafter as well. Agricultural tasks, the mainstay of the economy of ancient Egypt, were to be expected in Eternity. So content were the Egyptians with their lot, that the hoped-for farming differed in only one respect from that which they had known. The grain, in the fields of Iaru, grew a foot taller. The Afterlife was, for the

SEN-NEDJEM STANDING IN ADORATION BEFORE A SHRINE
Tomb of Sen-nedjem,
Theban necropolis (No. 1).
Dynasty XIX (1305–1200 B.C.)

Right
IRY-NUFER DRINKING FROM A POOL
Tomb of Iry-nufer,
Theban necropolis (No. 290).
Dynasty XIX (1305–1200 B.C.)

Egyptians, an extension of this life, and death was only the beginning of continued existence in familiar surroundings with family and friends. Such a view indicates that for the ancient Egyptians life was a pleasant, pleasurable experience which did not have to be exchanged for Paradise.

TOMB OF IRY-NUFER. *Dynasty XIX.* *pp. 133–138*

The Tomb of Iry-nufer is roughly contemporary with that of Sen-nedjem, both men having lived under Rameses II. The scene of IRY-NUFER DRINKING FROM A POOL (*p. 133*) over which spreads a palm tree is rendered with the same freedom as the floral representations in the Field of Iaru in Sen-nedjem's tomb. The somewhat awkward spreading of the branches of the tree results from the fact that this representation is painted on the outer edge of a vaulted ceiling. The bisection of the tree also requires an explanation. The artist wished to represent a scene consisting of a palm tree in the foreground, a rectangular pool in the middle distance, and Iry-nufer himself at the far edge of the pool. In this scheme, the need for visual clarity dictated that the trunk of the tree had to be bisected by Iry-nufer's body, which the artist deemed the most important element in the scene. This same concern is evident in the vignette showing ANUBIS ATTENDING THE MUMMY OF IRY-NUFER

Left
ANUBIS ATTENDING THE
MUMMY OF IRY-NUFER
Tomb of Iry-nufer,
Theban necropolis (No. 290).
Dynasty XIX (1305–1200 B.C.)

THE DIVINE COW
Tomb of Iry-nufer,
Theban necropolis (No. 290).
Dynasty XIX (1305–1200 B.C.)

(*p. 134*). Comparison between this scene and the analogous one in the Tomb of Sen-nedjem (p. 132) indicates that both are based on a similar model or pattern book. The anthropomorphic figure of Anubis is rendered in simultaneous views but the width of his shoulders has been contracted so that his arms appear in profile as they adjust the collar on the mummy coffin. The scene takes placed within a tented pavilion whose patterned textiles are placed behind the figures, to indicate that they are within the space thereby enclosed. In the picture of THE DIVINE COW (*p. 135*), the technique of applying plaster to the wall can be observed at the top of the illustration, where the thin stucco layer has fallen away to reveal the Nile mud with which the stone walls of the tomb were covered in an effort to obtain a smooth surface. This representation derives from Chapter 71 of *The Book of the Dead*, which contains a spell for the coming forth by day. At the left is the falcon who rises up from Nun, the mistress of Methwer, who symbolizes the celestial cow of the primeval age, lying over the original flood from which life began. Through the pluralistic conceits of Egyptian religion, renewed life is promised Iry-nufer in the way he will emerge at the dawn of the Afterlife to be resurrected in the new day. The water has been rotated ninety degrees so that the figures are shown on top of rather than alongside its edge. The heavenly cow is wrapped in the *sedeb*-cloth, has a sun disc on her horns, a flagellum at her back and a *menat* around her neck. The draughtsmanship is crisp and sure but within the formal traditions of all of the representations of this period. A third vignette from the same tomb shows IRY-NUFER AND HIS WIFE IN ADORATION BEFORE A CALF emerging from between two sycamore trees (*p.*

IRY-NUFER AND HIS WIFE
IN ADORATION BEFORE A CALF
Tomb of Iry-nufer,
Theban necropolis (No. 290),
Dynasty XIX (1305–1200 B.C.)

IRY-NUFER FACING A PHOENIX
Tomb of Iry-nufer,
Theban necropolis (No. 290).
Dynasty XIX (1305–1200 B.C.)

136). The pectoral around Iry-nufer's neck hangs in front of his near arm so that it is visible to the spectator; its white color intensifies that effect. The scene is yet another analogy to explain the resurrection of the deceased and adds an element of purity to the concept of resurrection. Here, the sun is depicted as emerging between twin sycamores, a natural phenomenon which is associated with a suckling calf, whose mouth is pure. This complex conceit revolves around the unsullied sun at dawn and the innocence of the deceased at the moment of his rebirth.

The unusual scene of IRY-NUFER FACING A PHOENIX on a papyrus barque (*above*), is an illustration of Chapter 83 of *The Book of the Dead*. Iry-nufer on the prow of the papyrus boat adores the phoenix while his son stands behind him ready to assist. The spell calls for transforming the deceased into a phoenix, which is sometimes taken to represent the *ba*, or soul, of either the God Re or Osiris. In either manifestation, the phoenix connotes the primeval deity of the world at its initial creation, and the return to the beginning of established cycles. By becoming a phoenix, the life cycle of the deceased begins anew as is appropriate for one just resurrected. The phoenix wears a sun disc and the sun itself appears to the right. The eye of Horus, symbolizing protection, guards the prow. The object immediately in front of Iry-nufer represents a crook to which a bundle, containing a knife which protrudes, has been strapped. It is the hieroglyph for "follower" and provides another of those visual puns of which the Egyptians were particularly fond. The final vignette selected from the Tomb of Iry-nufer represents THE SKY GODDESS NUT (*p. 138*). Although Nut can be represented as the celestial cow in the astronomical ceilings of the pharaohs of Dynasty XIX, she can

137

also be represented as a goddess whose protective wings envelop those dear to her. The use of reds and greens in this composition is exceedingly effective and detaches the figure from the more neutral yellow of the background.

TOMB OF NEFER-RENPET. *Dynasty XIX.* *pp. 139, 140*
The Tomb of Nefer-renpet harks back to the tombs of Dynasty XVIII. Nefer-renpet, who was also called Kenro, was scribe of the Treasury in the Estate of Amun-Re during the reign of Rameses II. In the row of four figures seated in the NICHE OF THE INNER ROOM (p. 139), Nefer-renpet appears as the second figure from the left. With him are seated his wife and two other figures, one of whom can be identified with certainty, namely the man to the right of Nefer-renpet, who represents Niay, the purification priest of Amun. All four figures wear similar wigs and broad collars; the men are bare chested and wear festive kilts with inscriptions running down the front. The women, at each end, wear long dresses. The niche is flanked by wide borders decorated with stylized lotus bouquets, called *ankhs* in Egyptian, again providing a pun

THE SKY GODDESS NUT
Tomb of Iry-nufer,
Theban necropolis (No. 290).
Dynasty XIX (1305–1200 B.C.)

on the sign of life. The multicolored ceiling may represent the cloth of a pavilion. The remaining wall space is decorated with scenes divided into two registers separated by several horizontal bands, some of which contain inscriptions.

GOLD-WEIGHING. TOMB OF NEFER-RENPET.
Dynasty XIX.

p. 140

In the inner room of the tomb are seven scenes depicting Kenro's activity as scribe in the Estate of Amun. One of his functions was to oversee the weighing of gold. Kenro, in the typical gossamer costume, sits on an elegantly crafted seat with his feet on a footstool. His far hand holds a scribal palette. With his left he gestures to two men, in smaller scale, who weigh the material. The left-hand figure is the scribe of Amun, named Bak-en-amen. He is preparing to record the weights which will balance the scales operated by the scale-keeper at the right. The figures of animals on the ground behind him are intended to represent the deben and its fractions, the unit of measurement

TOMB OF NEFER-RENPET
NICHE OF THE INNER ROOM
Theban necropolis (No. 178).
Reign of Rameses II, 1290–1220 B.C.

GOLD-WEIGHING
Tomb of Nefer-renpet,
Theban necropolis (No. 178).
Reign of Rameses II, 1290–1220 B.C.

used for volumes by the ancient Egyptians. These are placed on the scale's pan to balance the material being placed in the pan on the other side. The drawing style of these figures is in pure line, executed almost entirely with a fine brush, without much interior detail. The simple, sure line forms contours against the white background which evolve into expressive shapes. All of this is done *alla prima*, without any preliminary outline drawing in a technique related to vignettes painted on papyrus. As abbreviated as it may appear to be, this figural style is indebted to the art of the Ramesside court.

TOMB MOTIF OF THE JACKAL ANUBIS.

Dynasties XVIII and XIX.   *p. 139 & 141*

Tombs such as that of Nefer-hotep (p. 141), who served as chief scribe of Amun, probably under King Ay of Dynasty XVIII, provided the model for some of the later Dynasty XIX tombs. A comparison between the NICHE OF THE KHA-EM-HET TOMB (*p. 117*) and the NICHE IN THE TOMB OF NEFER-RENPET (*p. 139*) offers a good example of the phenomenon of archaizing. Both niches contain several figures in long wigs and gala costumes and both are provided with an upper frieze with confronted jackals in black on a white ground. In the earlier tomb (p. 141) this motif is large and centrally placed so that it dominates the space. In the tomb of Nefer-renpet, on the other hand, the motif assumes a more decorative quality in keeping with the smaller scope of the architectural plan (p. 139). Four jackals are used to fill the space, which is crowded with the addition of secondary motifs. The monumental quality of the earlier design has been abandoned in favor of a more purely decorative effect.

Below, and detail right
THE JACKAL ANUBIS
Niche of the Nefer-hotep Tomb,
Theban necropolis (No. 49).
Reign of Ay, 1352–1348 B.C.

TOMB OF PA-SHEDU, DEIR EL MEDINEH.

Dynasty XIX.   *p. 143*

The Tomb of Pa-shedu—an official who also held the position of Servant in the Place of Truth on the West—dates from the Ramesside Period and is related, in both its plan and decoration, to that of Iry-nufer (pp. 133ff). On the rear wall of the vaulted chamber, Pa-shedu is shown drinking from the sacred pool, just as in the Iry-nufer Tomb. But endeavoring to come to grips

Pp. 142–143
TOMB OF PA-SHEDU
Deir el-Medineh.
Theban necropolis (No. 3).
Dynasty XIX (1305–1200 B.C.)

THE STAR GODS
Tomb of Iry-nufer,
Theban necropolis (No. 290).
Dynasty XIX (1305–1200 B.C.)

with the same spatial problems, the artist of this vignette has placed the palm tree in front of the figure, and both the figure and the tree are on the top edge of the pool. In other respects the effect is identical. To the right, parents of the deceased and other relatives stand in three rows in attitudes of adoration. The tympanum is devoted to the sons of the deceased, named Menna and Kaha, adoring Ptah-Sokar in his manifestation as a falcon. Various gods of the Underworld line the vault and side walls of the tomb. Their attributes are standard.

THE STAR GODS. TOMB OF IRY-NUFER.
Dynasty XIX.   *Above*
On the ceiling of the tomb, the deceased is shown kneeling before the star gods and a sun disc shown in this detail. The five gods are represented in a series of overlapping profiles meant to indicate a row of seated figures. The lines on the throats as well as the prominent nostrils and pierced earlobes follow the convention of similar features in the tomb of Sety I.

VII UPPER EGYPT AND NUBIA

THE TEMPLE OF HORUS, EDFU. *Ptolemaic Dynasty.*

According to legend, Horus, in an attempt to avenge his father Osiris, waged one of his most important battles against his rival Seth at Edfu, the capital of the Second Nome of Upper Egypt. His divine consort was the goddess Hathor of Dendera. Horus and Hathor, on their respective festivals, journeyed to each other's sanctuaries. The Temple of Horus, at Edfu, like that of Hathor at Dendera (p. 45), was wreathed by a mudbrick wall and approached through monumental gateways. Built entirely during the Ptolemaic Period, begun under Ptolemy III Euergetes I in 237 B.C. and completed in 57 B.C., this sandstone temple is virtually intact and can quite rightly be regarded as the best preserved temple in Egypt.

The GREAT PYLON (*below*) serves as the entrance to the temple proper. To emphasize the central axis of this gateway, its twin towers were planned as mirror images of each other. Near each outer edge, King Ptolemy XII Neos Dionysos grasps a group of prisoners by the hair and brandishes a mace,

THE GREAT PYLON
Edfu.
Ptolemaic Dynasty (305–30 B.C.)

145

above which hovers Horus as a falcon, whose wings form a protective embrace behind the king. Facing the action stands Horus as a falcon-headed deity wearing the Double Crown. He is followed by Hathor, wearing the same crown, and represented as a graceful female figure in a tightly-fitting sheath dress which reveals the sensuous contour of her body. In the two upper registers, King Ptolemy XII is represented four times at the outer edges of the field making offerings to Horus and the deities in his entourage. The placement of the king relative to the deities on the pylon underlines the Egyptian concept of the temple. The gods dwell within. Consequently their backs are turned toward the entrance, as if to signify that they have just come from the inner sanctum. On the other hand, the king, who does not dwell within, is facing the entrance, to signify that he has arrived to pay homage. Once through the Pylon, the visitor finds himself in the COURT BEFORE THE VESTIBULE (*below*). The paving stones are still in place as are the thirty-two columns of the surrounding colonnade. The facade of the Vestibule and its intercolumnar slabs are comparable to those at Dendera. Here, a single statue of HORUS AS THE FALCON (*p.* 147) watches in silence over the courtyard, where in Antiquity on specific festivals the faithful were permitted to witness offerings made on a huge altar built for the occasion.

TEMPLE OF KALABSHA. *Ptolemaic Dynasty.* *p. 148*

Before the construction of the High Dam at Assuan, other smaller dams had been built spanning the Nile since 1898. The new dam, however, threatened to submerge the monuments of Nubia forever. In Antiquity the administra-

TEMPLE OF HORUS,
COURT BEFORE THE VESTIBULE
Edfu.
Ptolemaic Dynasty (305–30 B.C.)

HORUS AS THE FALCON
Statue with the Double Crown.
Entrance to the Vestibule,
Temple of Horus,
Edfu.
Ptolemaic Dynasty (305–30 B.C.)

tion of this region fluctuated between the Egyptians, who governed it as a province, and the Southerners, who were sovereign. Monuments constructed in this region are labeled Nubian, although many, like the temples of Kalabsha and Abu Simbel were built by Egyptians in traditionally Egyptian architectural idioms. Both of these temples were rescued from the rising waters of the Nile by the international campaign mounted by UNESCO in 1960. Like the Temples of Abu Simbel, the Temple of Kalabsha was dismantled, transported, and reassembled on a new site. Originally located some forty kilometers south of the High Dam, the temple now stands on a new site just one kilometer south of it. The temple dates from the reign of Ptolemy IX Soter II, and is roughly contemporary with the finishing touches on the Temple of Edfu, whose Vestibule it imitates. The long, low proportions at Edfu are here made shorter and taller. This results in isolating the component parts of the facade which are consequently not as harmoniously integrated. Although much of the temple was never finished, it is generally acknowledged as one of the finer examples of Egyptian temples in Nubia. The empty spaces left unfinished were appropriated by later generations for inscriptions which are of historical interest. On the rightmost screen wall is a decree of a Roman governor named Aurelius Besarion dating from the third century A.D., directing all owners of swine to remove their animals from the city of Kalabsha. More significant is the inscription of King Silko at the north corner of the facade. Silko was ruler of the Nobadae, the inhabitants of the

147

region around Kalabsha in the fifth century A.D. His inscription, in illiterate Greek, records his victory over the Blemmyes, a nomadic tribe which constantly threatened the region.

The sandstone of which the temple is built is extremely friable, subject to wear, and not conducive to holding a sharply carved line. Despite these limitations, some of the scenes in raised relief in the Vestibule are impressive. An examination of the bird-headed deity identified by Gauthier as the GOD MANDULIS (*p. 149*), a local Nubian god associated with the site of Kalabsha, reveals a mastery over the sandstone. The figure, consistent with long established Egyptian conventions, is represented in a series of simultaneous views, as is the guardian serpent before him.

A number of other temples have been moved from Nubia to other sites. To acknowledge the generosity of nations who rallied to the call of UNESCO,

TEMPLE OF KALABSHA
Court looking toward the Vestibule.
Ptolemaic Dynasty (305–30 B.C.)

the Egyptian government has given the rock-cut chapel or speos of Ellesyia to Italy, where it is reconstructed in the Egyptian Museum in Turin; the Temple of Debod now graces Madrid; the Temple of Taffeh is magnificently housed in Leiden; the Temple of Dendur adds to the Egyptian treasures of New York City; and the Gateway of the Kalabsha Temple is now in West Berlin.

TOMBS OF THE NOBLES OF ELEPHANTINE. *Dynasty XII.*

At an early date, the Egyptians seized upon the natural conditions of the Nile at the First Cataract as the logical southern frontier of their nation. Easily defended, the area was repeatedly the site of a garrison which also controlled the traffic of luxury goods from the heart of Africa into Egypt. Ivory was an important import and it is conjectured that Elephantine, the seat of the priesthood of the Ram God Khnum, is etymologically related to the ancient Egyptian word for "ivory-elephant." During the Middle Kingdom, powerful officials constructed their rock-cut tombs on the west bank of the Nile, just to the north of Elephantine.

Comparable to the sepulchers of Beni Hasan, the TOMB OF SA-RENPUT I (*p. 151*) a priest of Satis, titulary goddess of the region around Assuan, was

THE GOD MANDULIS
Sandstone relief in
Vestibule of the Temple of Kalabsha.
Ptolemaic Dynasty (305–30 B.C.)

149

constructed during the reign of Sesostris I during Dynasty XII. Although cut into the local stone, the jambs of the doorway are veneered with fine white limestone decorated with representations of SA-RENPUT I (*below*), seated in a chair whose legs are in the form of lions' feet resting on lathed casters. As emblems of authority, Sa-renput holds the long staff and shorter *kherep-*scepter. Clothed in a pleated, belted kilt, he wears a bracelet and a broad collar, and sports a fashionable goatee. The column of inscriptions directly over his head contains his name. The sunk relief carving, intended to catch the rays of the sun and enhance the modeling, is masterfully rendered. In a rare attempt to indicate spatial relationships, the artist has even depicted the heel of Sa-renput's foot visible from beneath the arch of the near foot. In the forecourt of the tomb, six pillars are decorated with representations of Sa-renput striding accompanied by his titles and names. In characteristic manner, the images, left and right, face the entrance proper and underline the Egyptian fidelity to balanced and symmetrical composition.

In the region of Assuan at the close of the Old Kingdom, an extremely powerful local potentate called Heka-ib ruled as a virtual independent kinglet. The concentration of such power in the hands of one individual was not uncom-

SA-RENPUT I
Sunk relief, limestone veneer on doorway of his Tomb,
Assuan (No. 36).
Dynasty XII (1970–1930 B.C.)

mon at that time, and is yet another indication of the strong decentralization of central authority which led to the collapse of the Old Kingdom. Despite his position, Heka-ib appears to have been a just official, sensitive to the needs of his constituents, to judge from the fact that the Egyptians of the Middle Kingdom subsequently dedicated a temple to his memory on Elephantine. Such a phenomenon was not uncommon in ancient Egypt. Great leaders, whose beneficial intercession among the affairs of their contemporaries was significant, made such a mark on the Egyptians that their memory was venerated and preserved. They could, it was thought, be invoked in times of trouble. This uniquely Egyptian phenomenon has been regarded by students of religion as the genesis by which canonization and sainthood evolved in the Early Christian Church. The TOMB OF HEKA-IB (*p. 152*) is literally choked with stelae left by pilgrims seeking intercession. In plan the tomb is irregular and contrasts with that of Sa-renput I. The Court and its Vestibule are of extremely tall proportions, as are also the two columns, which have a pronounced taper recalling the Classic module of later Greek temples. Set in antis, these columns frame the entrance to the tomb proper. But the wall decorations of OFFERING BEARERS (*p. 156*) in the tomb are clearly provincial.

TOMB OF SA-RENPUT I
Door jambs and Court of the Tomb, Assuan (No. 36).
Dynasty XII (1970–1930 B.C.)

They do not compare with the masterful painted scenes in the TOMB OF SA-RENPUT II (*p. 153*), an official who was the Overseer of all the priests of Khnum on Elephantine Island and Commander of the Garrison under Pharaoh Amenemhat II. The glory of this tomb, which is one of the largest in this necropolis and certainly the best preserved, lies in its colorful decoration. Each of the four pillars of the Small Hall is decorated with a striding figure of Sa-renput II over which, in a yellow band, appear his titles and names. The REAR NICHE (*p. 153*) shows Sa-renput II sitting at a table piled high with funerary offerings. To the right his son presents flowers. The rare appearance of an elephant used as a hieroglyph is clearly visible over the head of Sa-renput in both panels of decoration in this niche. In accordance with Egyptian convention, scale is used to indicate rank and the relative importance to one another of the various figures in any given scene. The hierarchy of Sa-renput, his wife, and then his son is preserved here. The figure of Sa-renput's wife on the left of the Rear Niche reveals the technique of the artists who decorated this tomb, since they failed to remove the grid

152

TOMB OF HEKA-IB
Columns at entrance of the Tomb, Assuan (No. 35d).
Late Old Kingdom (2290–2150 B.C.)

TOMB OF SA-RENPUT II
The court with its pillars and Rear Niche,
Assuan (No. 31).
Dynasty XII (1930–1895 B.C.)

Below
TOMB OF SA-RENPUT II
REAR NICHE
Assuan (No. 31).
Dynasty XII (1930–1895 B.C.)

153

with which the figure was drawn. This grid provided a checkerboard pattern 18 squares tall in which the proportions of the human figure could be drawn to meet the basic canon used in Pharaonic times. The use of blue as a background for the scenes anticipates its use later by the artists of Horemheb's royal tomb (pp. 54–59).

The Egyptians loved life and enjoyed many of the same pleasures in which we ourselves indulge. They were, for instance, devoted to pets, particularly dogs. This is indicated by the Two Dogs of Sa-renput I (*below*), which are depicted on the back wall of his tomb Court. They are given special prominence, being shown immediately behind his sandal-bearer in a place usually reserved for important family members or retainers. Investigations have even discovered over fifty names by which the ancient Egyptians called their pets. The characteristics of the dogs in Sa-renput's tomb have led some authorities to see a representation of the prized sloughi in the animal on the right.

These scenes are in marked contrast to the Offering Bearers in the Tomb of Heka-ib (*p. 156*). Executed toward the end of the Old Kingdom, when the authority of the central government had collapsed, the figural style seems retardataire and crude, as compared to that of the Tomb of Sa-renput I. Such comparisons, however, tend to ignore the cultural and artistic significance of the allegedly weaker style. The apparent disregard for artistic conventions allows for a certain freedom of expression which imbues these scenes with a charm universally associated with folk art. There is an aura of appealing freshness in the naive representations which is totally lacking in

TWO DOGS OF SA-RENPUT I
Sunk relief,
Back wall of Court,
Tomb of Sa-renput I,
Assuan (No. 36).
Dynasty XII (1970–1930 B.C.)

the more formal compositions of the Middle Kingdom tombs at Assuan.

The Assuan tombs are often complexes of two or more separate hypogea built in close proximity to one another and communicating with each other by common doorways within the hillside. Such is the case of Tomb 35d, which is connected with the Tomb of Heka-ib. The right wall of that complex is decorated with a scene of FOWLING IN THE MARSHES (above), depicting the owner spearing fish and hunting fowl with a throw stick. Such scenes are favorites at Assuan and several representations, with slight variations, are found in other tombs located here; but they lack the spontaneity of the representations in Tomb 35.

SARCOPHAGUS OF A MUMMIFIED RAM.
Ptolemaic Dynasty.   *p. 157*

The island of Elephantine was sacred to the ram-headed God Khnum, who in Egyptian mythology was believed to have created mankind by throwing clay onto a potter's wheel and modeling Man with his fingers. Although the ram served as the emblem of the God Khnum, the Egyptians did not revere every ram in their country as that god incarnate. They did, however, select one specific ram to serve that function and also developed a distinctly Egyptian practice which was frowned upon by the ancient Greeks. In order to gain the favor of Khnum or thank him for a wish granted, the faithful would procure a ram which would be appropriately embalmed and placed in an elaborate sarcophagus, made of gilded and painted gesso over papyrus or linen strips. Such mummified rams were left as "please" or "thank you" ex-votos in the extensive cemetery on Elephantine Island. The majority of these burials date from the Ptolemaic and Roman periods and were not restricted to Elphantine. Similar cemeteries of crocodiles are found at Kom Ombo, of ibises at Hermopolis, and of baboons at Saqqara.

THE GREAT TEMPLE OF RAMESES II, ABU SIMBEL.

Dynasty XIX.   *pp. 158–9*

Of all the monuments rescued by the appeal inaugurated by UNESCO, the most celebrated are the temples at Abu Simbel. Almost one thousand individuals were involved in the six-tiered operation which began in 1960 and ended on September 22, 1968, with the dedication of the temples on their new site. Refinements and finishing touches continued to occupy the salvage team until 1972. The South or Great Temple was built in honor of King Rameses II during Dynasty XIX. Cut into the living rock and of such colossal proportions, the structure appears to be a tour de force quite compatible with the megalomaniacal aspirations of the king there commemorated. The kings of Dynasty XIX, and particularly Rameses II, experienced a major threat to Egypt from the Hittites and witnessed the undermining of her influence abroad. In an effort to reassert their honor and celebrate the glory of Egypt, those kings embarked on building programs approaching the scope of the activity of the Pyramid Age. Grand architectural schemes could be construed as expressions of unlimited power. So it was that Rameses II

Above, and above left
OFFERING BEARERS
Tomb of Heka-ib,
Assuan (No. 35d).
Late Old Kingdom (2290–2150 B.C.)

selected a site deep in Nubia beneath the Tropic of Cancer on which to erect the grandest of his temples, which would inspire fear of his might and respect for his nation among the local inhabitants and all who travel the Nile northward to Egypt. In its plan, the Great Temple is simply a traditional Egyptian temple creatively arranged into a mountain rather than laid out on a plain. The four colossal statues of Rameses II stand before the facade which has been shaped into a pylon. The top of the pylon contains a frieze of twenty-four baboons, which the Egyptians believed screeched at dawn to welcome the rising sun god, here represented as a hawk-headed deity in the niche over the door. The temple was so laid out along a strict east-west axis that the rays of the sun would actually reach the innermost sanctuary at dawn, and illuminate the statues of Ptah, Amun, Rameses II deified, and Ra-Hor-akhte. The walls of the inner rooms are completely covered with painted relief decorations, which are conveniently divided into religious and secular representations. Of these, the battle scenes are the most interesting. They record the victories of Rameses II over a variety of foes and celebrate his glorious defeat of the Hittites at the Battle of Kadesh. The knowledge that that battle ended in a draw does not detract from the impression of awe, reaffirming Champollion's admiration of the ensemble.

Pp. 158–159
THE GREAT TEMPLE OF RAMESES II
Abu Simbel.
Dynasty XIX (1290–1220 B.C.)

SARCOPHAGUS OF MUMMIFIED RAM
Painted and gilded plaster.
From Cemetery of the Rams, Elephantine.
Ptolemaic Dynasty (305–30 B.C.)
Assuan Museum.

RAMESES II AS FIELD COMMANDER, SOUTH TEMPLE OF ABU SIMBEL. *Dynasty XIX.*

Egyptian temples were, at least from the New Kingdom on, decorated with scenes of battle, which expressed the fundamental philosophy of Egyptian religion toward the Pharaoh. The gods created the order and harmony in which the Egyptians could flourish. An attack on this order would result in chaos and confusion. The foreign foes of Egypt had to be held in check by Pharaoh's forces in order to maintain this order, and perpetuate the Egyptian way of life. In these representations of war, Pharaoh is the embodiment of stability and victory. He rides unmoved in his chariot despite the jostling ride and the rearing of his team. Amidst confusion and carnage, his aim remains steady and his arrows are accurately loosed. He is the image of order among the forces of chaos and the only one to whom the country can turn for support. Egypt was the Pharaoh, and the death of her last native king signaled the end of her civilization.

RAMESES II AS FIELD COMMANDER
Sunk relief.
From the Battle Scenes,
South Temple, Abu Simbel.
Dynasty XIX (1290–1220 B.C.)

HISTORY OF EGYPTOLOGY
AND MAPS OF EGYPT

Although the credit for inaugurating the first systematic study of ancient Egypt is ordinarily given to Napoleon and the team of scholars he took with him on his Egyptian campaign in 1798, the fascination with its monuments already existed in antiquity. Both the Greeks and the Romans traveled to Egypt, where in Ptolemaic and Roman times the Sphinx and the Great Pyramids were major tourist attractions. Pliny lists no less than twelve ancient writers who describe or mention the Giza necropolis, notable among whom was Herodotus who visited Egypt around the middle of the fifth century B.C. Book II of his famous *History* gives an extended and vivid account of his tour of the Nile Valley which is of considerable importance chiefly because of his keen firsthand observations. But many of the facts relating to what he describes are today of limited archaeological significance because they tended to be based on anecdotes he collected from chance encounters along the way rather than from official sources.

Nevertheless special value attaches to the writings of both Herodotus and of the later Greek geographer Strabo (b. ca. 63 B.C.) because they provide descriptions of monuments and sites now greatly deteriorated or no longer in existence. From them, for instance, we have a detailed description of the famous Egyptian Labyrinth, a complex architectural structure which was reported to contain in excess of 4,000 rooms. Used as a sepulchre and as an administrative center, the Labyrinth at Hawara in the Faiyum is today a vast area of splintered stone blocks. In Ptolemaic and early Roman times, a network of irrigation canals, based on patterns established during the Middle Kingdom, transformed the Faiyum into one of the most productive agricultural regions in Egypt.

The extended attention which both Strabo and his late Roman contemporary the Sicilian geographer Diodorus Siculus devote to Egypt in their general descriptions of the ancient world itself reflects the continuous interest the Romans had in the Pharaonic civilization. In fact, both the Greeks and the Romans identified major Egyptian deities with their own gods, and even absorbed some of the ancient religious beliefs, notably the cult of Isis.

As for the Egyptians themselves, there are many indications of active interest in their own past. Of major importance is Manetho's *History of Egypt*, written in Greek around 300 B.C., during the reign of either Ptolemy I or Ptolemy II. Manetho, a High Priest of the temple at Heliopolis, traces the history of his country from legendary times to 323 B.C., dividing it into thirty-one dynasties. This comprehensive account has come down to us in fragmentary form from the later writers Josephus and Eusebius, and his texts are confirmed by modern archeological findings, such as the lists of kings found inscribed on the Palermo Stone, the Turin Canon, and on a wall in the Temple of Sety I at Abydos.

Of legendary interest proving Egypt's respect for its past is the great granite stele, discovered in 1816 by T. B. Caviglia, between the paws of the Sphinx, erected by Tuthmosis IV about 1425 B.C. The inscription on the stele relates how the king, having been hunting in the desert near the Pyramids, went to sleep in the shade of the Sphinx and was admonished by a god in a dream to clear away the sand from around the base of the monument, carved a thousand years before. About 150 years later, a son of Rameses II, Prince Khaemwese (1304-1237 B.C.)—who has been called the first archeological antiquarian of ancient Egypt—left an inscription recording his restorations on the now sadly eroded pyramid of Unas at Saqqara, which dates from Dynasty V. Mention could also be made of an example from the seventh century B.C. of a relief depicting a pair of quarreling figures quite obviously copied from a wall painting in the tomb of Menna, decorated during Dynasty XVIII, some 700 years before (page 123).

These examples cannot be regarded simply as veneration for ancient things, in the conservatism which was such a basic characteristic of Egyptian life. The underlying tendency of archaizing, the conscious imitation of an earlier epoch by a subsequent dynasty, is a constant throughout ancient Egypt's long history. The monuments at Saqqara are even more dramatic examples of this archaizing tendency. The kings of Dynasty XXVI are believed to be responsible for the construction of the impressive quandrangular shaft in the Step Pyramid of King Djoser (page 29) which they commissioned to determine the exact plan of that tomb. The Late Period— Dynasty XXV through the Roman Period—is particularly noted for its attempts to resurrect ancient forms. The extremely deep burial shafts of certain Late Period tombs at Saqqara are apparently modeled on that of King Djoser.

With the arrival of the Greeks in large numbers in Egypt after her conquest by Alexander the Great, and the establishment of the Ptolemaic Dynasty in 305 B.C. by Ptolemy I Soter, the fabric of Egypt began to be altered. Two societies, separate and unequal, emerged. The cause of the Greeks was championed in certain cities, which enjoyed many privileges not accorded the native Egyptians. Official decrees, such as that of Ptolemy V Epiphanes found on the Rosetta Stone, were habitually recorded in Egyptian hieroglyphs, Demotic— a cursive form of the hieroglyphs—and in Greek, the official language of the Ptolemaic Dynasty. Despite these setbacks, the native Egyptians held tenaciously to their old traditions and beliefs, which were to be completely fragmented only by the Roman occupation begun in 30 B.C. When Egypt became a province of the Empire and the personal property of the emperor, the role of the pharaoh, the cornerstone of the religious and social life of Egypt, came to an end. Without royal commissions and royal workshops commissioned by a native pharaoh, traditions soon disappeared. The rise of Christianity, as a concomitant phenomenon, also hastened the end of Pharaonic civilization. The native Egyptians soon embraced this mystery cult and adopted a new script, called Coptic, with which to record their new faith. With the Islamic invasion in A.D. 639 (page 17), the last vestiges of most ancient Egypt were effaced as the Egyptians began to be an Islamic nation in the Medieval World.

Throughout the Middle Ages, in the Arab world as well as Christian Europe, Egypt was little more than a source of legends and folk tales. A tenth-century Arabic manuscript explains that the pyramids were built to preserve all human knowledge from loss in a universal deluge predicted by astrologers. In the Christian world, on the other hand, pilgrims to the Holy Land believed that the pyramids had been built by the Pharaoh at Joseph's suggestion to store grain for the years of famine, an imaginary interpretation of the *Old Testament* story which is depicted in a thirteenth-century mosaic in the basilica of San Marco, Venice.

During the Renaissance in Italy, when the unearthing of Greek and Roman sculptures created such a stir, there were also Egyptian monuments such as the obelisk brought to Rome by Constantius II in the fourth century A.D., and sculptures imported by the emperors to adorn their villas, to which attention now began to be directed. But these produced hardly more than fanciful speculations, like the abstruse interpretations of hieroglyphs in Francesco Colonna's allegorical love story, *Hypnerotomachia Poliphili* (published in 1499), and the esoteric scholarship of the Jesuit Athanasius Kircher (ca. 1650). Yet they reflect a pioneering intellectual curiosity about Egypt which in the eighteenth century was translated into voyages to the Near East and up the Nile, the antiquarian activity of amateurs, and collections of scattered objects and curios, all of which were part of the Romantic movement.

The account of one of those early travelers, *Voyage en Syrie et en Egypte*, published in 1787 by the Comte de Volney, is said to have been the inspiration for Napoleon's highly organized enterprise in taking along a commission of learned men to study the ancient remains in the Nile Valley, on his military campaign to Egypt in 1798. The moving spirit of this group—which included members of the French Institute—turned out to be the artist and diplomat Vivant Denon, a favorite in the court of Louis XV who was saved from the guillotine by his friend the painter J. L. David. After making a detailed survey of the Giza necropolis and examining the cemetery at Saqqara, Denon accompanied General Desaix in his march up the Nile as far as Assuan and the First Cataract, keeping records and making sketches at all the sites along the way.

Denon published his findings in *Voyage dans la Basse et Haute Egypte* (1802), later followed by the official publication of the French Institute, *Description de l'Egypte*, which appeared between 1809 and 1828 in thirty-six volumes. The first of these books created an instant sensation, and gave the impetus for travelers from all over Europe to go to Egypt, attracted not merely by eager curiosity but also by the chance of lucrative trade in antiquities. Typical of the period was the Italian adventurer G. B. Belzoni, who thoroughly explored Egypt (1816–19). The first to enter the pyramid of Cheops, he discovered seven tombs in the Valley of the Kings (page 50) and proceeded as far as Abu Simbel. Everywhere he acquired sculptures from temples and tombs, which he sold to collectors, mostly in England, including the alabaster sarcophagus of Sety I now in the Soane Museum, London.

The exhibition of Belzoni's discoveries which he organized in London in 1820 and then took to Paris was attended by enormous crowds. During this period of unhindered access to Egypt, under the open-handed policy of Mohammed Ali (1805–1848)—from whom it was easy to obtain a permit to dig—consuls, merchants and travelers all became collectors. Tombs were opened indiscriminately, and in the process almost as much was lost as found. It was at this time that the great collections of Egyptian art were made—the Drovetti, Salt, Anastasy and many others—which were to become the nuclei of museums in Europe.

Denon's spectacular account and the widespread interest it aroused would not have had such significant importance for the future of Egyptology had not the French scholar Jean-François Champollion in 1822 succeeded in deciphering the hieroglyphs on the famous Rosetta Stone, unearthed in the Delta at the village of the same name, by one of Bonaparte's officers. On discovery, its importance was immediately recognized, for in the Treaty of Capitulation in 1801, Napoleon was forced to hand the stone over to the British, although the French retained the right to publish its text. In the space of ten years after announcing his memorable solution in his celebrated *Lettre à M. Dacier*, Champollion managed to write his *Grammaire égyptienne* and *Grammaire hiéroglyphique* before his premature death in 1832. He also had the opportunity to apply his discovery on actual monuments, for between 1828 and 1830, with his younger protégé, the Italian Ippolito Rosellini, he led an expedition to Egypt, the results of which were published in his *Monuments de l'Egypte*. Having witnessed at first hand the alarming removal of antiquities from almost every major site then going on during this period, Champollion registered his apprehension by urging that a government body be set up to protect the monuments. But the proposal was ignored and the removal of antiquities continued. In 1831 Mohammed Ali offered to King Louis-Philippe the obelisk of Rameses II from the temple of Luxor, which was erected on the Place de la Concorde in Paris in 1836 (page 85).

In the wake of Champollion's discovery, it was left to the German Karl Richard Lepsius (1810–1884) to continue the scholarly exploration of Egypt. After studying under Champollion's pupil Ippolito Rosellini, and publishing a critical commentary on Champollion's system, he organized a large-scale expedition financed by King Friedrich Wilhelm IV of Prussia. For four years (1842–1846) Lepsius explored the Nile Valley and collected many objects which were to form the basis of the Berlin Museum. The results of the expedition were published in his famous twelve-volume survey, *Denkmaler aus Ägypten und Äthiopen* (1849–1859), which established the study of Egyptology on a firm scientific basis.

Slightly younger than Lepsius and one of the great figures of Egyptian archeology, Auguste Edouard Mariette (1821–1881) was sent to Egypt by the French government to acquire Coptic papyri for the Louvre. On arrival he became so impressed with the ancient monuments that his attention was completely diverted to exploration and excavation. At Saqqara in his search for the ancient site of Memphis, a sphinx's head protruding from the sand reminded him of a passage in Strabo describing the temple of Serapis (later called the

163

Serapeum), the burial ground of the sacred bulls of the God Apis. Clearing the ground with great difficulties over the space of four years he unearthed an avenue lined by almost 150 sphinxes which in Strabo's day were already half buried in sand. Mariette in 1850 finally reached the underground galleries of the tombs of the sacred Apis bulls in which were found sarcophagi, sculptures, and hundreds of stelae, left by pious pilgrims to these tombs.

Returning to France in 1854, Mariette was made assistant curator of the Louvre; but in 1858 he returned to Egypt and was appointed by Said Pasha as director of the newly organized Service des Antiquités, set up to promote and regulate all archeological activity, a post which he was to retain until his death in 1881. With an annual appropriation from the Egyptian government for research, he conducted excavations in Tanis, Memphis, Abydos and Thebes, everywhere making important discoveries. The objects collected from these excavations so impressed Ismail Pasha that Mariette was able to induce him to found the Egyptian Museum just outside Cairo at Boulak (1863). When some of the museum's holdings were exhibited in Paris in 1867, the Empress Eugénie asked the Khedive to give her the whole collection; but Mariette refused and henceforth would not allow any of the museum's most important objects to leave the country.

The pace and volume of Mariette's activities outstripped his ability to publish many of his discoveries, a lag which was largely compensated for by Gaston Maspero (1846–1916), his successor as director of the Service des Antiquités. Being already professor of Egyptian philology and archeology at the Collège de France, and having already published his great work, *Histoire ancienne des peuples de l'Orient*, Maspero was well qualified to establish Mariette's innovations on a firm basis. He instituted translations of the Pyramid Texts (discovered by Mariette), which were published in installments from 1882 on. And in a startling discovery, Maspero was responsible for salvaging the royal mummies from a funerary cache near Deir-el-Bahari—which for a long time had been a source of clandestine pillaging of antiquities—and for having the relics finally brought to the Cairo Museum for study. This event alone marked the advent of a new period in Egyptology, when controlled scientific excavation began to be substituted for the indiscriminate clearing of sites and removal of huge monuments for museum collections.

From 1881 on the Service des Antiquités ceased having a monopoly on archeological exploration, and permits began to be granted to qualified scholars of all countries. In England the Egypt Exploration Fund was established in 1882, "with a view to the further elucidation of the History and Arts of Ancient Egypt," and it was under the aegis of this foundation that William Flinders Petrie (1853–1942) inaugurated his revolutionary techniques of excavation. The most inconspicuous fragments scattered in the rubble of a site—isolated inscriptions on slabs or potherds, weapons, tools or pieces of jewelry—were now scrutinized as essential clues for dating and identification of a period or culture. Some of the outstanding discoveries stemming from Petrie's explorations include objects such as the famous Palette of King Narmer of Dynasty I, now in the Cairo Museum, an ivory statuette of

Cheops of Dynasty IV, now in the British Museum, the tiny gold and jeweled pectoral of Princess Sit-Hathor-Yunet, daughter of Sesostris II of Dynasty XII, now in The Metropolitan Museum of Art.

Petrie's systematic methods and standards of exploration, scrupulously followed by publication, thenceforth set the norm in Egypt, where not only French and English but also Italian, American and other Egyptologists now participate in excavations. The support for this multifarious activity came from such organizations as the Deutsche Orient Gesellschaft, the Institut d'Archéologie Orientale, the British School of Archaeology in Egypt and, in the United States, The Metropolitan Museum of Art in New York and the Oriental Institute in Chicago.

After Maspero, the Service des Antiquités, charged with granting permits to dig, continued under the direction of French scholars until 1952, when it was taken over by the Egyptian government under the Ministry of Culture. Already, by the law instituted in 1912, the concessions to excavate were no longer granted to individuals, but only to learned bodies; and excavators could only expect to take half of what they found, all other objects being reserved for the Cairo Museum.

Following Denon's initial survey of the Giza necropolis in 1799, when only the head of the Sphinx rose from the sands and rubble covered the entrances to the pyramids, it was not until 1815–1818 that a clearing operation was started by a Genoese sailor, T. B. Caviglia. He was followed by Belzoni in 1818, and Lepsius in 1842–43. But it was Mariette's extensive excavations between 1850 and 1880 which provided a definitive access to the site, accompanied by the record of the finds and translation of the inscriptions by Champollion, Rosellini and the English amateur Egyptologist, J. G. Wilkinson. Flinders Petrie's detailed measurements and observations of the Pyramids in 1880–82 gave the first rational explanation of how they were built, followed by studies by the German Ludwig Borchardt, the French archeologist J. P. Lauer, the Egyptian A. Fakhry. Of spectacular later finds at Giza, the so-called "Mycerinus Triads"—sculptures of that king between two deities—and the alabaster sarcophagus of Queen Hetep-heres, mother of Cheops, were both made by the American George A. Reisner; and the Solar Boat, from a pit near the south face of the Cheops Pyramid, was unearthed by the Egyptian Kamal El Mallakh (p. 21).

The extensive Saqqara necropolis with its tombs and impressive architectural remains ranging from Dynasties II, III, and IV, to the Ptolemaic period has been one of the most continuously explored sites of ancient Egypt (pp. 17–34). Mariette, who got his start in Egyptology with the previously mentioned discovery of the Serapeum (1850–54), had been preceded at Saqqara by the German H. M. von Minutoli, who was the first to excavate the underground burial chambers connected with King Djoser's Step Pyramid. He was followed by Perring and Vyse, then by Lepsius, Barsanti, and Maspero. From 1920 on, in excavations conducted by the Egyptian Antiquities Service, important investigations have been made at the site by Firth and Quibell and by J. P. Lauer. And in

1954, the unfinished pyramid of Sekhem-khet, Djoser's presumed successor, was discovered by the Egyptian archeologist Zakaria Goneim. In the Unas Pyramid, which is now in a completely ruined state, in 1937 Lauer discovered the well-preserved inscription recording the restoration of the pyramid by Rameses II's son, Prince Khaemwese (Dynasty XX). The year before his death in 1881, Mariette made the spectacular discovery of hieroglyphic inscriptions in the burial chamber of Pepy I's Pyramid, proving for the first time that inscriptions were to be found in pyramids, as well as in tombs.

Far more heterogeneous and varied than the archeological remains of Giza and Saqqara are those of the Theban necropolis and of Luxor and Karnak, which together have been called "the most valuable single cultural and artistic complex surviving from ancient times" (pp. 85–105). Already famous in Classical times—when Herodotus described its splendors and Alexander built sanctuaries here on whose walls his name was carved—Thebes continued to impress the Romans also, including Hadrian who visited Thebes in A.D. 130. The ancient name for the city which became the capital of Egypt in Dynasty XIII was *Was*; but the Greeks, impressed by its many pylons which recalled their own multi-gated city of Thebes, substituted that name for *Was*, which is still known as Thebes.

Although Thebes occurs throughout Medieval literature as a legendary place, its identity as a geographic reality became so completely forgotten that early travelers to Egypt had difficulty locating it. It was not until the eighteenth century that the ruins of Karnak and Luxor were recognized as those of ancient Thebes, by the Jesuit Claude Sicard (around 1710), and later by individual travelers, such as the Englishman Richard Pococke (in 1737–40).

After Denon's critical observation of the temples of Karnak and Luxor, the first to explore the Theban necropolis on the left bank of the Nile was Belzoni, who discovered no less than seven tombs in the Valley of the Kings, including that of Sety I, father of Rameses II (p. 62–64). Thebes was also one of the major sites to which Mariette, as director of the Service des Antiquités, devoted his explorations, particularly at Karnak and Deir-el-Bahari, which were published after his death in his *Monuments divers*, by his successor Gaston Maspero.

The excavations of the great temple of Queen Hatshepsut at Deir-el-Bahari were continued by the Swiss archeologist Edouard Naville, and later by the Americans Herbert E. Winlock and E. Lansing, of The Metropolitan Museum, New York. Work there continues under the direction of J. Lipinska, working with the Polish expedition. During this time also, Flinders Petrie, with the support of the Egyptian Exploration Fund, had been carrying on excavations in the temple complex of Rameses II, now called the Rameseum, with its reliefs showing the battle of Kadesh and the red granite colossus of the king (p. 101). In the meanwhile, starting in 1895, the systematic reconstruction of the temple of Amun-Re at Karnak was proceeding under the direction of Georges Albert Legrain, a member of the Institut Français d'Archéologie Orientale at Cairo. It was here, not far from the Sacred Lake, that G. Legrain in 1903 made the sensational discovery of the so-called Cachette, or Favissa at Karnak, which was a deep pit cut into the north court of the Seventh Pylon in the Temple of Amun at Karnak. Periodically, in antiquity, the Temple of Amun became cluttered with statues dedicated by the faithful. The priests who were charged with the maintenance of the temple had to make room for new dedications but could not simply throw away the older gifts. Their solution was to relegate those older dedications to this Cachette. In the course of three years of excavation, from 1903–1906, Legrain discovered over nine hundred stone statues and statuettes dating from Dynasty XX to the Ptolemaic Period. Most of these are now in the Cairo Museum.

Another French Egyptologist, Victor Loret, relying on Strabo's description of the royal tombs, had instituted systematic excavations of the hypogea in the Valley of the Kings which yielded important discoveries, including the tombs of Tuthmosis III and Amenhotep II (pp. 50–55). After Loret the exploration of the Valley was pursued by Howard Carter who, at the age of twenty-five, was appointed inspector-in-chief of monuments in Upper Egypt and Nubia by Gaston Maspero, who was then director of the Service des Antiquités. For a number of years the excavations were financed by the American Theodore M. Davis, who in the interest of science waived any share of the objects discovered, keeping only pieces not wanted by the Cairo Museum. When in 1912 Davis yielded the concession to dig to Lord Carnarvon, it was under the latter that Carter in 1922 discovered the tomb of Tutankhamun, the first pharaonic burial chamber to be found intact.

Excavations are still in progress in Egypt and many American institutions, including The Brooklyn Museum, are contributing to the progress of Egyptology. The Brooklyn Museum, under the direction of my colleague Richard Fazzini, has spent five seasons in the Precinct of the Goddess Mut, consort of Amun-Re, King of the Gods, and Lord of Thebes. This precinct, located at Karnak, has revealed at least five major structures and has begun to clarify our picture of that goddess, whose Sacred Lake, called the Isheru, is the most conspicuous feature of the site. It is estimated that over 500 granite statues of the Goddess Sakhmet, the leonine deity of grim aspect, represented seated or standing, like the example in the Temple of Ptah (p. 99), adorned the precinct. The exact number of these statues, their original placement, and the nature of their presence in this sanctuary remain questions awaiting answers. To date, the excavations of The Brooklyn Museum have uncovered monuments erected by Taharqa, the glorious king of the Kushite Dynasty (Dynasty XXV) whose prowess in war as an ally of the Children of Israel against the Assyrians is recorded in the Old Testament. By means of such excavations, our knowledge of ancient Egypt increases. And so long as scholars devote some of their time and energies to volumes such as those in this series, the public will continue to enjoy, understand, and appreciate the legacy of the world's longest, uninterrupted civilization.

Robert S. Bianchi,
THE BROOKLYN MUSEUM

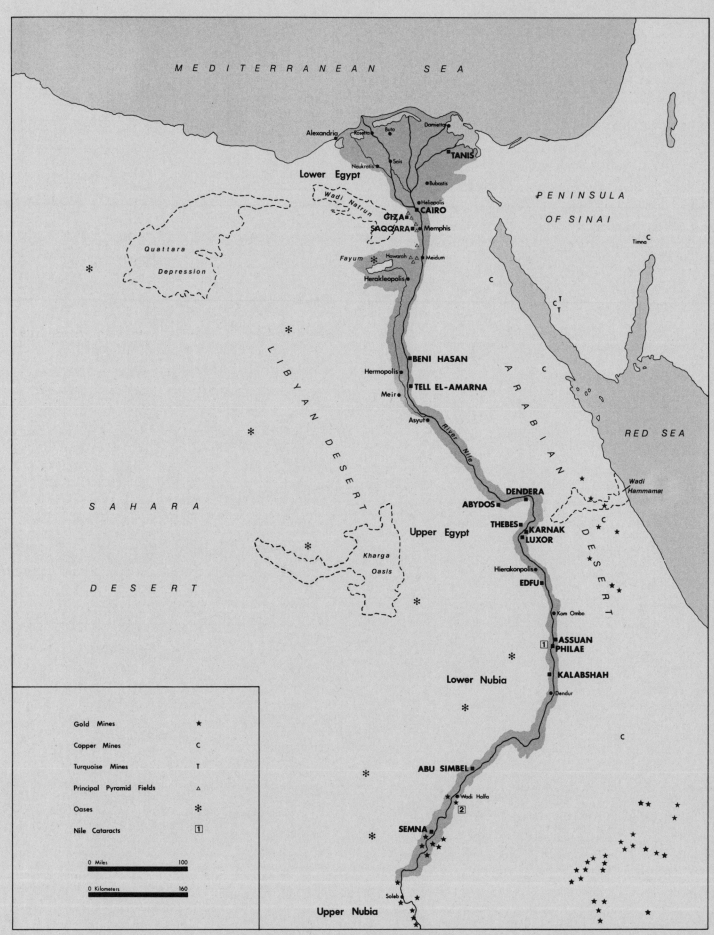

MEDITERRANEAN   SEA

Alexandria ● ● Rosetta ● Buto ● Damietta

TANIS ■

Lower Egypt

Naukratis ● ● Sais ● Bubastis

Wadi Natrun

PENINSULA

OF SINAI

Heliopolis ●

GIZA ■ △ CAIRO ■
SAQQARA ■ ● Memphis

Timna C

Quattara
Depression

△

Fayum ✳ Hawarah △ △ △ ● Meidum

Herakleopolis ●

✳

C

C   T
C   T
T

L   I   B   Y   A   N   D   E   S   E   R   T

✳

BENI HASAN ■

Hermopolis ●

TELL EL-AMARNA ■

Meir ●

A   R   A   B   I   A   N

RED SEA

Asyut ●

River Nile

✳

S   A   H   A   R   A

DENDERA ■

ABYDOS ■

★

Wadi
Hammamat

Kharga
Oasis

Upper Egypt

THEBES ■ ■ KARNAK
■ LUXOR

★

C

D   E   S   E   R   T

✳

Hierakonpolis ●

EDFU ■

★

D   E   S   E   R   T

★ ★

✳

Kom Ombo ●

✳

1 ■ ASSUAN
PHILAE

✳

Lower Nubia

■ KALABSHAH

● Dendur

✳

C

Gold Mines	★
Copper Mines	C
Turquoise Mines	T
Principal Pyramid Fields	△
Oases	✳
Nile Cataracts	1

✳

ABU SIMBEL ■

★ ● Wadi Halfa

★ ★

★

2

★

0 Miles — 100

0 Kilometers — 160

✳

SEMNA ■
★ ★
★ ★ ★

★ ★

★ ★
★ ★
★ ★ ★
★

★

● Soleb ★

★ ★

Upper Nubia

★ ★
★

★

MAP BY TRINA MANSFIELD BAYLES

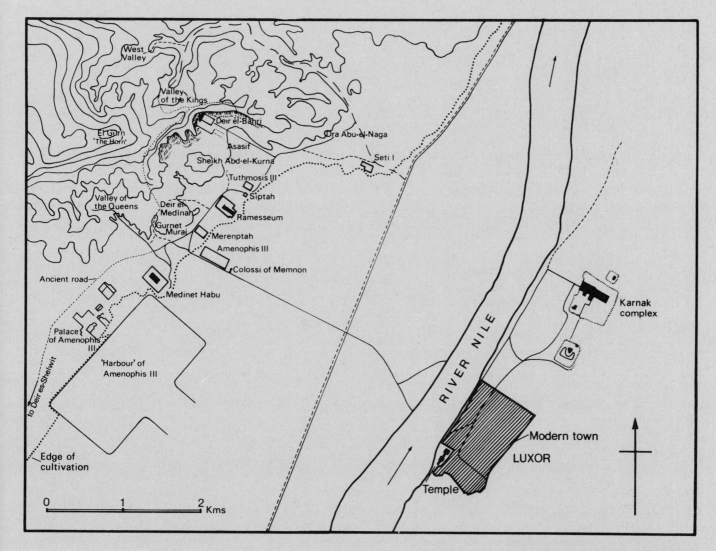

MAP OF THEBES

Reprinted from John Ruffle: The Egyptians.
Copyright 1977 by Phaidon Press Ltd., Oxford.
Used by permission of the publisher, Cornell
University Press.

MAP OF ANCIENT EGYPT

SELECTED BIBLIOGRAPHY

ALDRED, C.: *The Development of Ancient Egyptian Art from 3200 to 1315 B.C.* London, 1952.

BADAWY. A.: *Coptic Art and Archaeology.* Cambridge, Mass. 1978.

BAEDEKER, K.: *Egypt and the Sudan: Handbook for Travellers.* 8th rev. ed. New York, 1929.

BIANCHI, ROBERT S.: *Egyptian Treasures.* New York, 1978.

BREASTED, JAMES H.: *Development of Religion and Thought in Ancient Egypt.* New York, 1959.

CENIVAL, J.-L. DE: *Living Architecture: Egyptian.* New York, 1964.

DESROCHES-NOBLECOURT, CHRISTIANNE: *Tutankhamen.* New York Graphic, Boston, 1963.

EDWARDS, I. E. S.: *The Pyramids of Egypt.* Baltimore, 1961.

EMERY, W.: *Archaic Egypt.* Baltimore, 1961.

ENGLEBACH, R.: *Introduction to Egyptian Archaeology with Special Reference to the Egyptian Museum, Cairo.* Cairo, 1946.

ERMAN, A.: *The Ancient Egyptians: A Sourcebook of Their Writings.* Translated by A. M. Blackman, introduction by W. K. Simpson. New York, 1966.

FAKHRY, AHMED: *The Pyramids.* University of Chicago Press, Chicago, 1961.

FRANKFORT, HENRI: *Ancient Egyptian Religion.* New York, 1948.

GARDINER, A.: *Egyptian Grammer: Being an Introduction to the Study of Hieroglyphs.* 3rd ed., rev. London, 1957.

GARDINER, A.: *Egypt of the Pharaohs: An Introduction.* Oxford, 1961.

GARDINER, A.: *The History of the Middle East and the Aegean Region c. 1800–1380 B.C.* Cambridge Ancient History, vol. 2. Cambridge, 1975.

HAYES, W. C.: *The Scepter of Egypt: A Background for the Study of Egyptian Antiquities in the Metropolitan Museum of Art.* New York, 1953; Cambridge, Mass., 1959.

KEES, H.: *Ancient Egypt: A Cultural Topography.* Edited by T. G. H. James. Translated by I.F.D. Morrow. London, 1961.

LANGE, KURT, AND MAX HIRMER: *Egypt: Architecture, Sculpture, Painting in Three Thousand Years.* Phaidon, New York, 1968.

LONDON: BRITISH MUSEUM: *A General Introductory Guide to the Egyptian Collections.* 1964.

LUCAS, A.: *Ancient Egyptian Materials and Industries.* 4th ed., rev. by J. R. Harris. London, 1962.

MEKHITARIAN, ARPAG: *Egyptian Painting.* Skira, Geneva, 1954.

MICHALOWSKI, KAZIMIERZ: *Art of Ancient Egypt.* New York, 1968.

POSENER, G.: *Dictionary of Egyptian Civilization.* With the assistance of G. Sauneron and J. Yoyotte. New York, 1962.

REISNER, G. A.: *History of the Giza Necropolis.* Cambridge, Mass. 1955.

RIEFSTAHL, E.: *Thebes in the Time of Amunhotep III.* Norman, Okla., 1964.

SMITH, W. S.: *The Art and Architecture of Ancient Egypt.* Harmondsworth, England, 1958.

SMITH, W. S. *Interconnections in the Ancient Near East: A Study of the Relationships between the Art of Egypt, the Aegean, and Western Asia.* New Haven, Conn., 1965.

SMITH, W. S.: *Ancient Egypt as Represented in the Museum of Fine Arts, Boston.* 4th ed. rev. Boston, 1961.

WESSEL, K.: *Coptic Art.* London, 1965.

INDEX OF ILLUSTRATIONS

169

INDEX OF NAMES

Note: Italic Numbers refer to names mentioned in captions.

GENERAL INDEX